CUNNING EDGE

A 45-YEAR JOURNEY OF CONDUCTING
GLOBAL UNDERCOVER INVESTIGATIONS

Kim Marsh

◆ FriesenPress

One Printers Way
Altona, MB R0G 0B0
Canada

www.friesenpress.com

Copyright © 2022 by Kim Marsh
First Edition — 2022

Editor, Michael Mouland
Foreword by Rod Stamler

All rights reserved.

No part of this publication may be reproduced in any form, or by any means, electronic or mechanical, including photocopying, recording, or any information browsing, storage, or retrieval system, without permission in writing from FriesenPress.

All photos courtesy of the author except where otherwise credited.

Map on page 71, Voyage of the Blue Dawn, made with QGIS.

ISBN
978-1-03-912061-7 (Hardcover)
978-1-03-912060-0 (Paperback)
978-1-03-912062-4 (eBook)

1. Biography & autobiography, law enforcement

Distributed to the trade by The Ingram Book Company

To the memory of my brother, Peter. His dedication to the RCMP and the Undercover Program never faltered. He was a trailblazer and an inspiration to his colleagues and family. Peter packed more into one shortened life than most.

PRAISE FOR KIM MARSH

... gives the reader a front row seat in the theater of clandestine investigations by both police and private investigators. Marsh's first-hand experience as an undercover operative, educator, and manager takes you across the globe with tales that will impress readers with their degree of daring and ingenuity. Woven into the stories are powerful insights on personal development, human behavior and psychology, and business management. These are the fruits of [his] wealth of experience, which ranges from a twenty-five-year distinguished career as a law enforcement officer with the RCMP to a further twenty-two years as an accomplished entrepreneur and business executive. This book has a lot to offer to a wide spectrum of readers. And it is an entertaining read.

Martin S. Kenney
Managing Partner
Martin Kenney & Co., Solicitors
International Fraud and Asset Recovery

Raw, riveting: a must-read for cops transitioning from the beat to the business world.

Fabian Dawson
Editor, Author, Filmmaker
Recipient, Lifetime Achievement Award, Postmedia

A rare and insightful look into the training and cases of an undercover operative. Kim Marsh takes us on an international journey into the life of an undercover officer and the lessons and insights he learned in his forty-five-year career fight against drugs and crime.

Robert Silbering
New York City Special Narcotics Prosecutor (1991–1997)

This... memoir of [an] over-forty-five-year odyssey of RCMP undercover operations and the development of an equally intriguing and related subsequent business life is timely. Much of the public, media, and politicians, as well as police/intelligence officials in liberal democracies, typically have been overwhelmed and bewildered by the inherent complexities of business-related criminal schemes, particularly those related to global organized crime.

Marsh's professional life stages engage the reader in a straightforward personal narrative of cases that illustrate and help explain how our current and unprecedented state [of] international business criminality evolved. Whether or not one agrees fully with Marsh's views on the inadequacies of Canada's political and judicial systems, readers will find his insight into this form of criminal enterprise fascinating. It is reminiscent of the visceral atmosphere of Martin Scorsese's movies, blended with personal history and easily accessible writing. In addition, for readers involved or interested in business opportunities, Marsh provides important thematic points at the beginning of the key related business chapters.

Raymond Corrado, Ph.D.
Professor, School of Criminology
Director, Institute on Violence, Terrorism & Security
Simon Fraser University

I have known Kim since his posting in Miami and worked with him in policing and business. His biography gives an insightful look at the works of the RCMP—one of the world's top police forces—and its innovative use of undercover work and international liaison officers. From humble beginnings, Kim shows how attention to detail and hard work made him a very successful police officer and businessman. This book is an excellent read for anyone wishing to advance in their chosen career, showing that with hard work and dedication you can achieve whatever you wish.

Terry Burke
Former Detective Superintendent
New Scotland Yard

TABLE OF CONTENTS

PRAISE FOR KIM MARSH v
FOREWORD xi
INTRODUCTION xv
CHAPTER ONE
LONDON FROM DRUID: THE ROAD LESS TRAVELED 3
CHAPTER TWO
LUCK OF THE DRAW (EARLY DAYS) 11
    Introduction to Undercover Work 13
    Dark Operators Within our Midst 17
CHAPTER THREE
STINT AT RCMP HEADQUARTERS & ONWARD 19
    "Mr. Big" 22
    Off to Miami & Working with the DEA 26
CHAPTER FOUR
DEVELOPING THE NETWORK & AVOIDING THE PITFALLS ... 29
    Working with Informants 33
    Big Problems 37
    Drug Ties to the Mob & Inside Corruption 38
CHAPTER FIVE
PRESIDENTS & DESPERADOS 41
    Switching Sides 43
    Touchdown & Takedown 45
    The Trial 46
    A Deadly Message 47
    The Panamanian Connection 48
CHAPTER SIX
LONDON & BEYOND 53

Welcome to the Wild East 55
The Land of Trusting Fools 57
The Russians are Coming 59

CHAPTER SEVEN
THE BLUE DAWN INVESTIGATION **65**
Electronic Trackers 66
A Hotel a Day Keeps the Doctor Away 67
The Takedown 71

CHAPTER EIGHT
MAKING THE LEAP & THE EARLY WINS **77**
Advantages of My Former Career 79
Undercover Again 80
Smoking Out the Criminals 81
One Big Client 83
To Sell or Not to Sell? 84

CHAPTER NINE
THE IPSA ROLLER COASTER RIDE **87**
Saving the Company 88
Clearing Our Client's Name 91
Flight Takes Off with No Confirmed Seat for IPSA 94
CYA—Always 97
A New Revenue Stream 99

CHAPTER TEN
THE LONDON-CARIBBEAN EXPERIENCE **101**
Eat What You Kill 102
The Past Catches Up 103

CHAPTER ELEVEN
THE EVOLUTION FROM A PRIVATE TO PUBLIC COMPANY .. **113**
Establishing a Global Brand 115
A Deal is Hatched 117
Carving Off IPSA 119
The Deal Closes 120

EPILOGUE **123**
Further Reading **125**

FOREWORD

Between 1981 and 1987, I was the Director of the National Drug Enforcement Program at the Royal Canadian Mounted Police Headquarters in Ottawa. The officers and members of the headquarters Drug Enforcement Branch oversaw all major national and international drug investigations in Canada and provided training and assistance to the drug sections in each province.

Because of the nature of illicit drug trafficking, many of the investigations required the services of undercover operators. The branch was responsible for the selection and training of undercover operators. Over the years, the RCMP had experienced many problems associated with long-term undercover investigative work. Members assigned to these duties often ended up with PTSD and related psychiatric disorders that threatened the successful outcome of the prosecution of the drug offenders that were being charged as a result of the undercover operation.

Kim Marsh was assigned to the Drug Enforcement Branch in 1983. He was transferred to the National Undercover Section and became responsible for the selection and training of undercover operators across Canada. It soon became evident that Kim was a highly dedicated professional police officer, who took over his new duties determined to develop a new and improved Undercover Program.

His insight and dedication produced one of the most professional undercover programs ever developed in the western police world. The program achieved immediate success. His new concept, involving careful selection and training of undercover operators, has been copied by most major police forces in Canada.

Kim continued to manage the Undercover Program until his transfer to Miami in 1988. This position was created as part of the Canadian national drug strategy that positioned RCMP liaison officers to major cities in the United States. Kim was assigned to Miami, where he worked with the United States Drug Enforcement Agency. He represented the RCMP in major drug trafficking and money laundering investigations that related to Canada.

In 1988, I retired from the RCMP and joined the accounting firm of KPMG. Several years later, as chairman of an international forensic investigative firm, I had the opportunity of meeting Kim again. At that time, he was a member of the Canadian High Commission in the United Kingdom as the RCMP Liaison Officer. Kim continued as a member of the RCMP until his retirement in 1999.

In 1999, Kim began his private sector career and established a very successful investigative firm that was subsequently acquired by a major international corporation. It was obvious that Kim had excelled very quickly in the private corporate investigative world.

In the years that followed, I had a number of opportunities to work with Kim on major corporate investigation cases. Kim is a very effective private investigator. His knowledge, honesty, and integrity resulted in his investigative firm becoming a leader in the industry.

This book is an insightful account of Kim's accomplishments, in both the RCMP and his subsequent work in the private sector. His background and experience in dealing with police investigations, which he has outlined, provide an understanding of how and why undercover operations are conducted by police organizations. He also demonstrates some of the problems and difficulties police officers experience in carrying out their duties in the criminal underworld.

Kim's many years of experience in the international corporate investigative world have provided a special insight into how corporate and private investigations are carried out. Kim shares his experience and skill as a corporate fraud investigator, his knowledge of international money laundering, and details on the offshore banking system.

Kim's journey from his days in Druid, Saskatchewan to his days as an undercover expert in the RCMP, his achievements in the corporate world, along with his travels from Moscow to Libya, make an interesting and captivating account of the life of an international investigator.

Rodney Stamler, LL.B.
Assistant Commissioner RCMP (retired)

INTRODUCTION

As I reflect upon my career in the public service and later on my career in the private sector, much of it seems a bit surreal. I started out in this world as a small-town Saskatchewan boy with little consideration for my future. An opportunity to join the Royal Canadian Mounted Police (RCMP) presented itself when I was not even considering a career in law enforcement. My life experiences in both the public and private sectors were unconventional on many levels. Being from rural Saskatchewan and growing up in a small hamlet with the unlikely name Druid, I envisioned my life policing small towns in the prairies. As things turned out, I took a much different path.

After completing twenty-five years of service with the RCMP, I ventured out into the private sector, again with an incomplete picture of my direction but with the desire to transfer my skills into business opportunities. The result was another interesting adventure that took me on a second global tour, begat a successful business enterprise, and culminated in setting standards for compliance in the Immigrant Investor Industry.

I joined the RCMP in 1973, when the requirements to qualify for the force included being male and single, a British subject or Canadian citizen living in Canada, being between five feet, eight inches and six feet, five inches in height, possessing a grade eleven education or higher, and having the ability to speak either French or English. That in itself is surreal, considering the world we live in today. I joined at the age of nineteen in 1973, and after completing basic training in Regina in January of 1974, I was heading to my first posting in Chilliwack, British Columbia.

Starting my policing career in Chilliwack was fortuitous for several reasons, including meeting one particular person who dramatically altered my career path. Ken Alford was several years senior to me and worked in drug enforcement. He recognized in me some qualities that suggested that I would be a good candidate for undercover work. After getting through the selection process and training, I commenced my new duties as an undercover operator, shaping the direction of my career with the RCMP. I spent eight years intermittently doing covert work around the country, and eventually that led to being moved to headquarters in Ottawa, where I became responsible for the selection and training of operatives for the National Undercover Program.

Again, I was fortunate to be in the right place at the right time. Rod Stamler was the officer-in-charge of the National Undercover Program and recognized potential in my ability to adapt to different situations, and I was moved to Miami as a liaison officer. I was the first Mountie to be posted full-time to Miami, and there were many challenges getting the office established. Along with the challenges came opportunities and the beginning of a global network of contacts. Between 1988 and 1992, my office was housed in the Drug Enforcement Administration building where I worked several cases featured in this book.

After Miami, I had a cross-posting to London in an established office where I worked with a colleague. I arrived in 1992, and a year later, our office was given geographical responsibilities to cover the Former Soviet Union (FSU), as the country was just opening up to the western world. In many ways, this was a very different experience from the one in Miami. During the five years I spent in London, my global reach extended to another level. I worked with law enforcement representatives from many countries stationed in the UK and traveled extensively throughout Europe and the FSU.

After my time working abroad, I received my last RCMP posting to Vancouver, where I ran an organized crime target team for a couple of years. During the last three months of my service, I worked twelve hours daily on a maritime contraband smuggling case. The investigation was named Project "E" Profit, and the smuggling vessel involved was called the *Blue Dawn*, from which we seized several tons of hashish. It was a great finale to my law enforcement career and an interesting story.

My service in the RCMP was far from conventional, and during most of it I was as a single man. Without a family of my own to consider, I was able to accept transfers and fully immerse myself in the job. For these opportunities

I am grateful, as it was fortuitous to have lived in some interesting places and through some interesting times.

My venture into the private sector was pretty typical in retrospect: I had no clients and little revenue for the first few months. The initial experience was peppered with self-doubt, and I questioned my decision to venture off on my own. But my vision of what I wanted remained intact and kept me going. My original company, West Coast Investigations & Consulting, eventually grew to yield $500 thousand in annual revenues after four years. Early wins included getting Microsoft as a client, conducting a complex investigation at Vancouver International Airport, and teaming up with another firm to conduct "big tobacco" investigations.

Then an unexpected acquisition offer came from an American entity, IPSA International. After much deliberation, I chose to sell and started as managing director with the company in Vancouver. During my fifteen years with IPSA International, I moved up to being president of the firm. Then, in 2017, we were acquired by Exiger, a risk management firm based in New York.

Entering into long-term covert work early into my policing service was unique for a number of reasons. First, most people in law enforcement were not employed by a department that had an established undercover program, and the RCMP was a leader in this category. Then you had to be spotted by someone who understood covert work. Also, you had to get through the selection process and training before being sent on an assignment. Fortunately, all of the stars lined up for me. I was also a single person who was prepared to go away on extensive assignments. When I started working undercover, assignments would normally be several months in duration, and you did not return to your home turf until the job was completed. Having this kind of opportunity toughened you up mentally very quickly and taught you how to be resourceful. Long-term covert work certainly was not a good fit for many of my colleagues for various reasons.

Another unique aspect of my journey was being fortunate to live through the early days of covert work being undertaken by the RCMP. In the 1970s and into the 1980s the recruiting of operatives was directed toward junior officers when there was a greater demand for operatives than a supply. Thus, there was no shortage of opportunities to go on assignments. That all started to change in the 1990s. Few people are sent out on long-term assignments any longer.

Having mentors such as Rod Stamler to provide guidance when moving into the private sector was a bonus. Because of my confidence in using undercover techniques, I did not hesitate to make the necessary moves that allowed me to develop interesting cases, some of which were highly successful. I am not the first person to use the undercover technique in the private sector, but few have used it for as long in such a variety of situations. My hope is that by reading about my journey I am able to pass on knowledge, insight, and motivations for others who will navigate their own paths in this intriguing and fascinating world.

This book weaves many stories together that transpired across numerous continents, with many of the adventures involving the use of undercover skills. The reader will certainly be entertained by how the investigative objectives were pursued while learning the effectiveness of the technique. As readers will discover, the covert technique can be interwoven into an array of scenarios, and this book provides some details on how this was done.

The book also offers insight into past eras that have come and gone and can never be relived. Reading the book will provide a glimpse as to what it was like to be part of a life that most will not be fortunate enough to experience. Hopefully it will also inspire others to evolve from law enforcement to corporate investigations in the private sector.

In this book, I've profiled some of the most memorable investigations I was involved in over the years. It describes the many law enforcement skills that I acquired on the job. These skills were useful in enhancing my business acumen and mitigating risk, as well as solving problems for my clients. As business tools, these skills also became instrumental in developing new business and managing client expectations. It is my hope that in reading this book you will take away something useful and also find the stories engaging.

Notes:

When appropriate I have identified people by name; however, the book includes some stories where I do not feel comfortable disclosing who was involved or where disclosure could cause security issues for some individuals.

Unless otherwise noted, all currencies mentioned within these pages are expressed in United States dollars.

PART ONE
THE FIRST ACT

CHAPTER ONE
LONDON FROM DRUID: THE ROAD LESS TRAVELED

- Appreciate the advantages of hard work and how to tough it out.
- Take stock of your heritage.
- Learn to take on responsibilities.

The forty-five-year journey recounted in this book begins in a place called Druid. Where is Druid, and more importantly, how did I end up there? I moved to Druid in 1956 with my family. At the time it was a hamlet with a population of 100 people, located in the province of Saskatchewan. I lived there for most of my formative years. The population of Druid is now zero.

London is on the complete opposite side of the spectrum to Druid. I have spent eight years of my life living and working in London in my different careers, and my work has resulted in 100 or more trips to the UK between 1990 and 2020. London is the crossroads of the world, partly because of Britain's global expansion over the centuries; plus, it is the focus of the English-speaking world. There are a wide spectrum of countries and people represented in London, and this mixture creates an atmosphere of creativity and culture. There is also a dark, sinister side to London that stems from it being a global financial center that attracts extreme wealth, creating opportunities for money launderers, fraudsters, and other nefarious characters. This in turn creates business opportunities for people such as myself to pursue the characters lurking in the shadows.

Everyone has a family story, and I always thought mine was somewhat unique. The journeys taken by my ancestors were not easy, but they did build character and inner strength. I like to think some of it was passed on to me.

The first contact my family had with Saskatchewan was through my maternal grandfather, who was given a one-way ticket to the Dominion of Canada from the United Kingdom, compliments of a child migration scheme. The purpose of the scheme was to send boys off to the colonies—Australia, Canada, New Zealand, and South Africa—to work on the farms. It was hatched in 1869 and resulted in one hundred thousand boys being relocated over several decades. The boys were from impoverished families or were orphaned. The scheme lessened the financial burden on the UK while providing much-needed laborers in the colonies. My grandfather was fourteen years of age when he arrived in 1904, and originally he lived on a farm near Franklin, Manitoba, which is located west of Winnipeg.

Eventually, my grandfather was offered employment with Canadian Pacific Railway (CPR), and he relocated to Moose Jaw, Saskatchewan. In the early twentieth century, the railways were critical to the development of western Canada, where small towns were springing up throughout the area.

Along came World War I. Locomotive engineers were in demand in Europe as troops and supplies needed to be shuttled to and from the front lines. CPR released engineers to join the Canadian Overseas Expeditionary Force, and in 1917, my grandfather signed up. He was posted to Audruicq, Pas-de-Calais, France near the Belgium border. It was here that my maternal grandparents met and married. My grandmother was a French national. After the war was over, they moved back to Moose Jaw where they raised four children, the youngest being my mother Jean.

Circa 1956. This photograph depicts Druid when we moved there in 1956 when I was three years old. The station house is on the right side along the tracks. All but a couple of the buildings have since been razed.

During WWI, locomotive engineers were in demand in Europe as troops and supplies needed to be shuttled to and from the front lines. CPR released engineers to join the Canadian Overseas Expeditionary Force, and in 1917, my maternal grandfather, front row, second on the left, signed up. He was posted to Audruicq, Pas-de-Calais, France near the Belgium border.

Another world war came along, which resulted in many young men and women meeting and starting lives together. This is what happened with my parents. My father, Eric, joined the Royal Air Force (RAF), and as part of the "British Commonwealth Air Training Plan" he was sent for pilot training to Saskatchewan, where he met my mother in Moose Jaw.

Eric was British, born and raised in India, where my grandfather, Keith Marsh, was serving with the British Army. The Marsh family consisted of multi-generational army people. While living in London, I did some research at the British Museum and located numerous vital statistics records associated with my grandfather, great-uncles, uncle, and my father. My grandfather was also born in India, and he joined the British Army just a few days shy of his fifteenth birthday. He spent two stints in the trenches in Europe and was awarded the Military Medal for Bravery. He was a big man, a serious boxer, and was heavyweight boxing champ of the British Army and Indian Army from 1922–26. He was Anglo-Indian mixed race, and a recent analysis of my DNA showed me to be 14 percent Indian.

My father, Eric, was British, born and raised in India, where my grandfather, Keith Marsh, was serving with the British Army. The Marsh family consisted of multi-generational army people. He spent two stints in the trenches in Europe and was awarded the Military Medal for Bravery. He was a big man, a serious boxer, and was heavyweight boxing champ of the British Army and Indian Army from 1922–26.

After Eric completed his training and obtained his "wings," he returned to the UK, where he was attached to a Spitfire squadron. For the last year of the war, he was posted to the Far East, spending time in Ceylon (Sri Lanka) and Malaysia. My parents had maintained contact, and my mother accepted a proposal via letter, traveled to the UK, and married my father in Bedford, England. In 1947, they emigrated to Moose Jaw with my eldest sister in tow.

My father Eric joined the Royal Air Force (RAF), and as part of the "British Commonwealth Air Training Plan" he was sent for pilot training to Saskatchewan, where he met my mother in Moose Jaw. After Eric completed his training and obtained his "wings," he returned to the UK, where he was attached to a Spitfire squadron. For the last year of the war, he was posted to the Far East, spending time in Ceylon (Sri Lanka) and Malaysia.

Most of my mother's immediate family lived in Moose Jaw, including my grandparents, and it would seem to have been the logical place to reside. But that was not to be. Eric began his career with the CPR as a station agent and, after a couple of moves to remote hamlets, we ended up in Druid, where the anchor was thrown out for fifteen years. The upside to living in Druid was that Dodsland was only one mile away. It was a community of 500 people with schools, a hospital, and the normal assortment of businesses. Druid did not have sewer and water; we burned coal to heat the station house, had a crank-style phone on a party line, and Morse code telegraph was still being used up until 1971. I am proud of my Saskatchewan roots, but Druid was on the margins of the world and its location presented serious limitations.

A strong work ethic was instilled into my brother and me at an early age. We had the standard duties around the house, including fetching drinking water, hauling out coal ashes, hauling out the toilet pail, and working in the large vegetable garden, plus we worked for local farmers and business owners to earn pocket money. Along with these chores, we assisted our father with the dray business. The dray business involved delivering goods that came to the station house and needed to be transported to consignees. By 1965, goods were no longer coming via train but rather via transport truck from Saskatoon, the nearest city. Normally, a local person would be contracted to do the deliveries, but given that my brother and I were able to assist, my father decided to buy a truck and take on the delivery contract which was separate from running the station house. Shortly after taking on the contract, Eric blew out his back doing some heavy lifting; it was up to my brother, Peter, and I to take up the slack. We would come home from school to stacked-up goods ready for delivery to the various local businesses. These included deliveries to the local pub and liquor store. So, there we were, twelve and fourteen years old, with the legal drinking age twenty-one and driving age sixteen, hauling cases and kegs of beer to the hotel pub and boxes of hard booze to the liquor store. On a heavy day we could be working until eight o'clock at night.

One of our days of delivering has always stuck with me. It was in the spring, I believe April, and the rain had been coming down heavily for several hours. Rain in the spring, when the local farmers were sowing their crops, was certainly an inconvenience, but it did bring the always-needed moisture. Saskatchewan is a dry, arid region.

While the farmers were waiting for the rain to stop, many would head to town and spend the day(s) in the local pub. On this particular day of note, Peter and I had the truck loaded with cases and kegs of beer. We were tired and anxious to get the consignment off-loaded so we could head home for a much-needed meal. We were tired and drenched to the bone. We had the truck backed up to the trapdoor that opened into the hotel refrigerator, but the innkeeper could not hear us banging on the door in an attempt to beckon his attention. The trap door could only be opened from inside the walk-in refrigerator. Peter told me to go around to the front of the hotel, enter the pub, and get the attention of the innkeeper. Upon opening the front door, I was hit with a waft of stale beer and cigarette smoke. At the same time all eyes were on me—the twelve-year-old kid who should not have been there. It was my first venture into a drinking establishment, albeit not to partake in consuming, but rather delivering the alcohol.

As boys, my brother, left, and I would come home from school to deliver goods to various local businesses. Later, I would follow in Peter's footsteps as an RCMP recruit. We are pictured here during our time on the undercover training course.

I was itching to get high school finished with and leave Druid. My chance came in June 1971, two days after finishing grade twelve. The station houses were being closed down throughout the province, including the one in Druid, and my parents moved to Rosetown, Saskatchewan, with my younger sister, where railway business was done by driving between different communities. The small-town prairie railway business and the communities were disappearing quickly, and within a few more years many of the villages had dwindled considerably.

When school was out, I went with a few of my friends to a local lake community for a couple days of partying, returning home where I packed my belonging into a couple of boxes. This was the first step in my journey.

I spent the summer working at the Dodsland hardware store and living at the owner's residence. In September, I moved to Lethbridge, a small city 300 miles away in southern Alberta, where I went to college and played a year of junior hockey. While there, my brother was training at the RCMP academy in Regina. He was scheduled to graduate in October 1971, and my mother made contact with me, suggesting that I attend the ceremony, which I wasn't keen on doing. However, she was insistent, and sent the money for the nine-hour bus ride to get there. My mother knew I was adrift and was hoping that my attendance at the graduation ceremony might spark an interest in following the same path as my brother. Her plan worked.

The CPR station in Druid, Saskatchewan, where the adventure began.

CHAPTER TWO
LUCK OF THE DRAW (EARLY DAYS)

- Seizing opportunities that are presented along the way.
- Challenging yourself and avoiding complacency.
- Getting out of your comfort zone.
- Following your instincts when things do not smell right.

At my mother's behest, I found myself attending my brother's graduation from the RCMP police academy. The graduation ceremony occurred at the training center in Regina, where basic training took place and is the location of the original headquarters for the RCMP. Originally the force was known as the North West Mounted Police, created in 1873 to bring civil order to the western part of Canada. The name changed to the Royal North West Mounted Police in 1904 and eventually became the Royal Canadian Mounted Police in 1920. Recruits came in from around the country to make up thirty-two-person troops who were put through rigorous training on their way to becoming police officers. The RCMP had a world-renowned reputation for being difficult to qualify for, and their motto was *Maintien le droit* (Maintain the Law).

Something about the graduation exercises appealed to me. I was rudderless and looking for some adventure, and I submitted an application to join in June 1972 and managed to get through the vetting process. I signed up for training in Regina on July 16, 1973, the centenary year for the RCMP.

Training days were long, starting at six o'clock with a morning parade and continuing with a full day of classes and physical activities including drill, swimming, weight training, and self-defense. In the evenings, you would complete your academic assignments and meticulously maintain your kit. My troop mates came from across the country and were for the most part close to twenty years of age and male. Some of the recruits were overcome by homesickness. I remember one poor chap who was out of sorts in Regina. His name was Wayne Power, and he was a Newfoundlander. He was going through culture shock and not coping well with being in Regina and approached me near the end of the day about one week into training.

I was staring out the window at nothing in particular when Wayne asked me "if I ever got used to it." I said I was unsure of what he was referring to, and he replied, "The flatness." My response was that I did not know anything else, so had nothing to adjust to. The landscape around Regina is very flat, and a local joke was that you could watch your dog run away for three days. In those days, you signed up for five years, and if you wanted out of the force earlier it was necessary to purchase your exit. Wayne put in his purchase papers a week later. Mercilessly, Wayne Power was given a new name by his troop mates: it was "Will Power."

At basic training, we were housed military-style in thirty-two-person dorms, and I actually enjoyed my time there. Like most of my troop mates, it was not easy for me some days, due to my smaller stature, but I toughened up both mentally and physically, and the six months went by quickly. There was great camaraderie and banter in the dorm, and it suited my personality. Near the end of training, you were given three choices as to what provinces you wanted to be posted to. I did not pick British Columbia but ended up being posted there. This was a stroke of blind luck for me. The RCMP had a number of different roles for its recruits throughout the country. In every province or territory, except for Ontario and Quebec, they did regular, uniformed, patrol work after completing training, which provided a solid foundation for becoming an effective police officer.

On many levels, British Columbia has more to offer than much of the country: it has an abundance of natural beauty and a less severe climate than the prairies. My first posting was to Chilliwack, which had a population of sixty thousand when I arrived. It is located sixty miles east of Vancouver, in the Fraser Valley. There were several other young Mounties posted there, and at the time, it was a training detachment for people coming out of Regina.

Chilliwack was a place where you could do some good, solid, police work, enjoy your days off with your colleagues, and adapt to a new life. At that time my annual pay as a third-class constable was $7,600; you did not join the RCMP for the money. To save money, I roomed with three other Mounties who were living in a rented house. There were not many dull days around the house that we dubbed "the snake pit" during the fifteen months I lived there. We had some great parties that were frequented by many of the locals. In 1974, the RCMP had a significant policy change allowing women to join, and there was no requirement to be single for the first two years of service. However, the "single" part was not an issue for me, as it was my marital status for the next twenty years.

INTRODUCTION TO UNDERCOVER WORK

Ken Alford, a drug squad officer, moved into the house for a few months in the later part of 1974. He was senior to me and had been doing undercover work around the country. We had talked about his covert work, but there was never any discussion about me having an interest in going down that path. Then, in June 1975, I was transferred to Penticton, which is in the Okanagan Valley that runs up the middle of the province. It was known for its fruit orchards then, and now is a top wine-producing area. I was working general patrol duty and was approached by the undercover coordinator for British Columbia, who asked if I was interested in pursuing long-term covert work. Alford had put my name forward as someone who may have what it takes to do this kind of work. Meeting Alford was a game changer for me. I was getting bored in Penticton, as there was not much criminal activity in the area. In fact, I had started looking over the fence, and I was considering taking a break from police work to do some extensive traveling.

Doing undercover work is different from being a specialized plainclothes officer. The RCMP was the first police force to initiate undercover selection and training in Canada and is known as a leader in the global law enforcement community for its selection process. The laws in Canada allow the gathering of evidence through deception, and one Mountie based in Vancouver, Abe Snidanko, recognized the potential for this investigative technique. Most crime is investigated after the fact, meaning the crime has happened and the police try to figure things out and gather evidence. With undercover investigations, you infiltrate crime groups, which allows undercover investigators to be on the scene when nefarious acts are being planned and committed. It is a very effective method, but it has its risks. Juxtaposed with Snidanko having the foresight to develop the undercover technique was a legal system that allowed undercover evidence. Entrapment of a suspect is not an acceptable way of gathering evidence. Entrapment occurs when the person of interest is tricked by an undercover operator into committing a crime that would not have normally taken place. It is similar to coercing a person into confessing to a crime they did not commit. Proper care and control of the Undercover Program from its inception has allowed law enforcement in Canada to avoid this pitfall. Courts in western Europe and elsewhere have not taken the same position as Canada for gathering evidence, thus restricting law enforcement from conducting covert investigations at the same level.

Snidanko initially trained people in Vancouver on a regional basis, but eventually, the program was taken nationally, with the training coordinated out of headquarters in Ottawa. Snidanko had moved on to Hong Kong as a liaison officer before I came along in 1975. I was interviewed in Kelowna, not far from Penticton, by Doug Ewing, who was doing a cross-country trip considering potential recruits for upcoming training courses. Four of us interviewed for a spot, and I was the only one recommended to participate. In early November, I completed what turned out to be my last uniform shift and headed off for Ottawa.

The course format split operators, who were trained to be inside a criminal organization, from handlers, who would manage long-term investigations. All of the operators were single, with less than five years on the job. Being an operator was not conducive to being married; you were expected to take on a new identity and relocate to new surroundings around the country. I had been in the field only twenty-two months upon attending the course and had little knowledge about the seedy side of urban centers. My life experiences up to this point did not include spending much time in larger urban cities, and certainly not in the dodgy parts. As the course progressed, we were sent on nightly exercises where we mingled with the local drug dealers in an attempt to purchase contraband. It was like being thrown into the deep end of the swimming pool without having spent much time in the water. This exposure was intimidating in the beginning, but as the course moved along, I quickly gained confidence.

My brother, Peter, was also on the course. Siblings trained together was a first for the program. Training on the same course as my brother provided me with some comfort in the beginning, as he was both blood and a familiar face. Peter had already been involved in undercover work as an operator before the course in the 1970s when he worked on a drug enforcement investigative unit in Victoria, British Columbia, and he had a couple more years of service than I did. Peter was a single-minded person, which allowed him to focus fully on what he was doing. This attribute in his personality also led to him not being overly communicative; not much information was passed on to me before and during the training. In the end, the people managing the course did not believe it would be best to send us on a long-term assignment together. I am surmising they sensed some sibling rivalry (which could have been accurate), but I did not think it would be a hindrance. Not surprisingly, no one was too interested in my opinion.

The course was extremely intense and challenging. We did not attend a police-training center but were housed in a hotel, the purpose being to get operators out of their police mentality and surroundings. Operators were put to work developing a new persona plus adjusting behaviors and communication skills. There were lectures to attend during the day, followed by evenings in the local bars fraternizing with the criminal element until midnight. You would then return to the hotel where detailed notes were written up. This was a daily routine, and the demands were cranked up as you moved along through training, giving instructors the opportunity to assess the aptitude of the candidates.

I managed to perform well on the course. Unknown to me, a handler attending the course, Ken St. Germain, was talent spotting and looking for operators to work in Toronto where he was posted. St. Germain approached me on assessment day, and at the end of the course, I was assigned to a long-term job in Toronto. This made me a bit anxious, but I had signed up for the long haul, and I began preparing myself mentally for the next challenge.

At the end of the undercover course, I was assigned to a long-term job in Toronto, along with people from the RCMP, the Toronto Metropolitan Police, and the Ontario Provincial Police (OPP). The author is seen in the front row, middle, wearing a floral-patterned shirt. Pat Kelly is pictured in the back row, on the extreme left.

Garry Clement was also picked for the Toronto operation. He had been on the course ahead of me. We were both housed in a three-bedroom apartment located at the Don Valley Parkway and Eglinton Avenue on the east side of the city. Our targets were mid-level drug dealers who were trafficking in cocaine, methamphetamine, and heroin. St. Germain was my main handler, and Clement was teamed up with Pat Kelly. Kelly was a high-flying drug squad Mountie who was an operator with a different persona than most of his colleagues. He was urbane, had a black belt in judo, and spoke Spanish. He was somewhat aloof from the rest of the group. The personnel on the project included twelve people from the RCMP, the Toronto Metropolitan Police, and the Ontario Provincial Police (OPP). Clement and I were the operators, along with one fellow from the OPP, Mike Hayes. We all ground it out separately while living full-time in the apartment, commonly referred to as "the shack."

I started out slowly, but eventually got things going, and in the end, we were all buying multiple ounces of drugs from an array of dealers, some of which were beyond mid-level dealers. The project culminated in a round-up of approximately 100 offenders in June 1976.

There were a number of interesting experiences during the months I was in Toronto, but one occurrence stands out, and it involved Kelly. About two months into the job, Kelly approached me and asked me what I knew about cocaine (normally we had little dialogue with each other). My response was, "Only what they taught me on the undercover course." He came to the shack the next day when most of the team were out on the road and proceeded to produce three one-ounce bags of cocaine, telling me one was 30 percent pure, one 60 percent, and one 90 percent. He then demonstrated some methods to determine purity using the water, burn, and feel test. Operators were instructed to never use drugs, a cardinal sin. I never did, and Kelly did not suggest that I try some, but I was confused as to what he was sharing with me. My first thought was, *this is stuff I learned on the training course*, and second, *where did he get these bags of cocaine?* Upon finishing his mentoring, he asked that I not mention this to St. Germain or others, as they might see it as interference. I agreed not to say anything but found the whole interaction perplexing.

DARK OPERATORS WITHIN OUR MIDST

Kelly turned out to be an infamous Mountie for many reasons. After our job was finished up, with Clement and I returning to British Columbia, things started to unravel for Kelly. First his house burned down, and the OPP were investigating it as an arson. Kelly collected on the insurance payout and bought a high-end condominium at the Palace Pier on the edge of Lake Ontario. He was also on law enforcement's radar for a number of other reasons and eventually quit the RCMP unceremoniously. Kelly lived a lifestyle that was well beyond his means, and then his wife mysteriously fell from the balcony of their condominium in March 1981. He became the prime suspect, was convicted of first-degree murder, and was sentenced to twenty-five years.

There are many dark stories about Kelly, and there is little doubt in my mind he was a nefarious character before joining the RCMP. Unfortunately, he was not vetted properly when he applied to join up.

One reason for telling the Kelly story is to demonstrate some of the pitfalls of working in the murky world of undercover operations. Normally it is the criminal element one needs to watch out for, but in this case, there was a criminal in our midst. I am not entirely sure to this day why Kelly did the cocaine demonstration with me. Perhaps he was planning something or testing me. Many years later, when posted in Miami, I ran into someone who *was* testing me. More about that in Chapter Four.

After completing the undercover operation in Toronto, I returned to British Columbia, where I was attached to a drug squad in Chilliwack and then one in Vancouver. Leading a nomadic life, I continued to undertake operations intermittently for eight years around the country, in Calgary, Halifax, the Yukon, and throughout British Columbia.

Another lucky break for my career came my way when I was assigned to work on an investigative unit with the Vancouver drug squad that was being run by Abe Snidanko, who created the RCMP Undercover Program. He was an iconic person for me, a great boss from whom I learned much, a tremendous supporter of my career, and he eventually became a good friend. Meeting interesting people like Snidanko is a common theme in my line of work, and we will meet many of his ilk throughout this book.

It was 1983, and I had completed ten years on the job. During those ten years, a lot had been packed in, allowing me to develop a strong foundation while growing my confidence. At the time, I was not aware that the years of undercover and drug enforcement duties honed skill sets that would not only take me through the next fifteen years of policing, but more importantly, would prepare me for my second act in the private sector. When doing undercover work, you learn to assess people and situations quickly, you are constantly managing risk, you learn to handle rejection from targets, and all the time, you learn how to develop strategies that will enhance success. Working with informants and agents who are criminals provides opportunities to learn things that cannot be gleaned without direct experience. Managing cunning, deceitful people is no easy task.

CHAPTER THREE
STINT AT RCMP HEADQUARTERS & ONWARD

- The finer techniques of interviewing: a skill set that transcends policing.
- Learning quickly that I was not cut out for institutional politics.
- The media and journalists, a different perspective learned.
- The "Mr. Big" investigative technique, and how to think outside of the box.
- The challenges of opening a new office in Miami.

In July 1983, I was promoted and moved to RCMP headquarters in Ottawa, where my job was to select and train operators who were interested in the RCMP National Undercover Program. Until 1988, I was the primary person in the RCMP tasked with the selection, training, placement, and re-entry follow-up of officers who were interested in doing covert work. In some cases, the candidate would already be working on plainclothes units, but for the most part, they came from the uniform ranks. The candidate would have been screened at the divisional level first, and then I conducted a second interview. If the candidate was successful with the second interview, then they would be scheduled to participate in a training course.

There were three undercover courses held annually, normally in Montreal, Toronto, and Vancouver. The training venue would be in a hotel, and my job entailed traveling across the country three times a year to fill the course openings. The three-week course would include twelve potential operators and twelve handlers as candidates. While I found parts of my experience in

Ottawa working in HQ stifling and bureaucratic, there were many takeaways that served me well when I did go back into the field, and also when I retired from the RCMP and moved to the private sector.

During my tenure as the undercover coordinator, I partnered with Ron Lewis at the Training and Development Branch, and together we would put on the courses. Lewis would manage and coordinate the course; I was the primary trainer, and others would be brought in to do lectures and assist with street exercises. It was a very intense three weeks, and given that the course was also part of the selection process, not all candidates would be recommended to pursue this specialized type of work. During the course, a candidate would continually be assessed on their performance in the classroom as well as on the street. The successful operator candidates would then return to their divisional duties. They would be included in the HQ pool of operators who would fill position requests coming in from the divisions. The undercover pool would total no more than two hundred active operators—not a lot of people, considering there were approximately sixteen thousand police officers in the RCMP during those years.

Prior to arriving in HQ, my predecessor had introduced a psychological component to the program. Dr. Michael Girodo, a professor at the University of Ottawa, would lecture for a full day, teaching candidates on how to deal with the stresses of the job, of which there were many. Girodo also interviewed people who had been doing undercover work in an effort to learn more about how stress negatively impacted operators' personal lives. He was also learning from past experiences to enhance the selection process and the program.

It had become evident to Girodo that the selection interview process had some shortcomings and there was a need to improve on how decisions were made in determining who was the right fit for undercover work. The negative effects of doing long-term covert work can emerge in many forms, including alcohol abuse, a dysfunctional domestic life, and poor personal and career decisions. In extreme cases, there were cases of suicides and substance abuse. The time to address the ugly side effects of covert duties was overdue.

I worked intermittently for a year with Girodo, traveling across the country and interviewing course candidates. Girodo continued to gather data while teaching me new skill sets. We switched from "selecting *in* to selecting *out*."

The text below is a quote from the *Interview and Selection Procedure Manual* prepared by Girodo:

> In the many years the RCMP had been involved in training, placing, monitoring, and studying the performance of operators in the field, certain important conclusions and general considerations emerged. One, in particular, concerns the underlying talent which is sought in potential operators. Some people can show a high degree of dissimulation and role-playing talent, often with extraordinary expertise in persuasiveness, ingratiation, and manipulation. When these performances and behaviours originate in underlying abilities and traits, they are often associated with the emergence of the very problems and difficulties referred to previously. The preference is to select applicants who can demonstrate an aptitude for learning dissimulation and role-playing through training and structured experiences, rather than select candidates who can perform this way out of personality predispositions.

Looking back, the years working at HQ were a critical time for my own self-development. The tutoring I received from Girodo helped to hone my interviewing skills and taught me how to identify and recognize inherent personality traits in individuals. Learning how to interview effectively is critical for law enforcement, for obvious reasons, but there are other benefits as well. It teaches you how to interpret a verbal response while observing non-verbal signs. An example of physical behavior is constant sighing or yawning during an interview. This is a clear sign of an emotional response and most likely indicates someone suffering from anxiety. An emotional or neurotic person is not a good candidate for undercover work, and historically, operators possessing this characteristic develop other disorders. I also learned how to identify answers that were untruthful. This is invaluable knowledge and instrumental when trying to assess a person or situation.

Most people are not going to have the opportunity to work one-on-one with a psychologist for the length of time I did, but learning how to interview effectively is important for managers in both public and private sectors. In subsequent years, I have continued to work and develop this skill by attending Certified Fraud Examiner courses, as well as other training sessions. Like any skill, one must practice to maintain what has been learned.

"MR. BIG"

Over the years, numerous law enforcement agencies and police departments from around the world have understudied the RCMP Undercover Program and taken what they have learned to enhance their own initiatives at home. The initial concept of going undercover in the RCMP was conceived in the Vancouver area. An outtake from this technique is known as the "Mr. Big." This technique was also conceived in British Columbia, primarily in Vancouver. British Columbia has the largest representation of RCMP officers in Canada with approximately five thousand officers. The next-largest division would be Alberta, then Saskatchewan and Manitoba. The two provinces with the largest populations, Ontario and Quebec, have provincial police departments and thus a much lesser need for RCMP officers. In Ontario and Quebec, the RCMP does not have the mandate to investigate serious criminal code offenses such as homicides.

The Mr. Big technique was conceived, developed, and authenticated as an effective covert investigative technique. Its humble beginnings involved a scenario where it became evident in a post-operation review that the "person of interest" came very close to admitting to murdering his girlfriend. The opportunity to gain a confession from this particular person was missed, but it spawned the idea that, with more preparation, better results could have been obtained.

When a homicide investigation had strong circumstantial evidence implicating a suspect, a plan would be hatched allowing covert operators to meet the subject and befriend them. The scenarios would leave the impression with the suspect that the new friends were part of an organized crime group, and often they would disclose information about crimes committed. The admission alone was never the only evidence to support a murder conviction. It was part of a large evidence package, corroborated by DNA, eyewitnesses, leaky alibis, and other circumstantial evidence.

Convictions have been challenged many times up to the Supreme Court of Canada, resulting in support of the convictions while providing guidelines to be followed by the law enforcement community.

My older brother, Peter, is credited along with others in developing this investigative procedure. Peter worked on the undercover unit in Vancouver for many years, eventually becoming the officer-in-charge. A close friend and colleague of Peter was Al Haslett, an undercover operator who excelled at the Mr. Big scenarios and covert work in general. Over the years, hundreds of cold case murders were solved, and in some cases the operatives were able to exonerate people who were originally seen as suspects. In numerous cases the target took the operatives to gravesites where victims were buried or would provide details that only the killer would know.

One famous case involved two Canadians, Atif Rafay and Sebastian Burns, who were convicted of brutally murdering Rafay's parents and his handicapped sister who lived in Bellevue, Washington. The victims were clubbed to death. Investigators in Washington State strongly suspected Rafay and Burns were responsible for the killings, but they could not obtain enough evidence to support charges.

The suspects lived in the Vancouver area, and the covert unit was engaged. After playing out several scenarios, the two provided clear details on how the crime was committed and their motivation. They wanted the life insurance money to produce a movie. Both were convicted of first-degree murder in Washington State and are serving life sentences.

There are some people who still contend the two were wrongfully convicted, and there is a Netflix documentary series based on the case called "The Confession Tapes." In speaking with Haslett, who was the primary operator assigned to the case and who was playing the Mr. Big role, he points out some obvious gaps in the contention of innocence. The convicted felons knew the order of killings and how they were done. Both of these details were only known by the homicide investigators and had not been disclosed to the public or the operators. Second, Rafay's DNA was found in the shower of the house where the murders took place. Third, a witness testified that Rafay and Burns discussed their plan to execute the victims with him prior to the murders. The witness, Jimmy Miyoshi, was living in Vancouver at the time of the conversation but did not participate as he was otherwise occupied on the night the murders were to take place. Miyoshi testified about the murder plot at the trial.

No convictions have been reversed since the technique was first used in Canada in the early 1990s, and many countries have copied the Canadian model.

Sadly, my brother, Peter, died of a blood disease in August 2009. Approximately eight hundred people from across Canada and the USA attended his memorial.

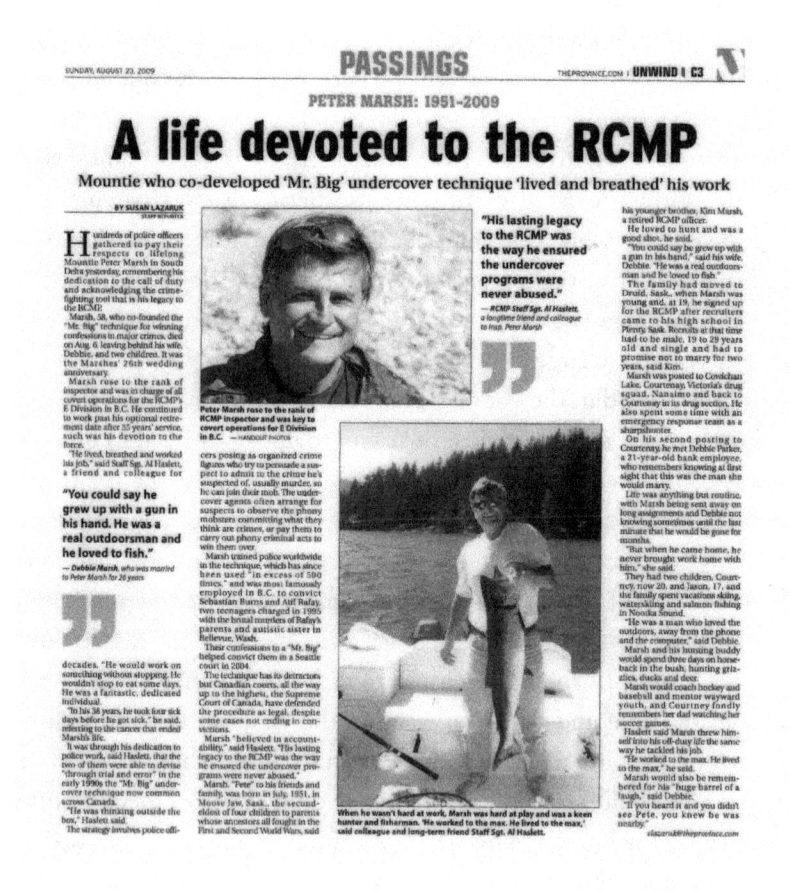

> My older brother Peter is credited along with others in developing the "Mr. Big" investigative technique that led to solving hundreds of cold case murders. Sadly, my brother, Peter, died of a blood disease in August 2009. Approximately eight hundred people from across Canada and the USA attended his memorial.

For many years, the "Mr. Big" technique has been successfully used, and there was little media or public attention given to it. This began to change in the early 2000s, when Fabian Dawson, a journalist, came forward with an interest in writing about the program. Dawson approached me when I was already retired from the RCMP, and eventually our discussions led to whether I would consider facilitating an introduction to Haslett and Peter. After some consideration, Peter and Haslett agreed to a meeting at a local restaurant in July 2005. After dinner, we retired to my condominium deck and continued our dialogue for several hours on a warm summer evening. Dawson gained their trust and arranged further meetings with my brother and his team. RCMP management agreed to allow Dawson a peek into the inner sanctum of the covert unit, with the objective of writing about the program to enlighten the public about the RCMP's work. This was a win-win story for the force and the media and is an example of how law enforcement and the media can cooperate. A multi-faceted story was published in *The Province* in September 2009, and everyone came away pleased with the piece. Often the relationship between the police and the press is contentious. Journalists can be aggressive when trying to pursue a story—that is their job. Learning to work harmoniously with the media is important for law enforcement and for the private sector. Stories can be told without causing damage to any of the parties involved.

I have engaged journalists on numerous occasions to assist with private investigations. Journalists are generally resourceful and capable when it comes to locating sources who can be used to corroborate inquiries. In today's world, with extensive privacy legislation in place, much information is not public and accessible only through the courts. Being able to mine human-sourced information, whether covertly or openly, is critical to moving many investigations forward.

An Ontario Superior Court judge I know is a former Mountie and trained undercover operator. In a recent discussion with him, he revealed that he uses regularly the skills learned from his undercover experiences to assess people and their evidence in his role as a judge.

The undercover technique is multi-faceted. The experience while in my job in HQ prepared me for future engagements in the police as well as in the private sector. I recently learned the Undercover Program is having problems attracting candidates who want to get involved in this kind of policing. I am assuming this is a direct correlation to the type of person entering law enforcement as a career. This is unfortunate on many levels.

OFF TO MIAMI & WORKING WITH THE DEA

During the mid-1980s, the Mulroney government initiated a federal strategy to deal with the illicit drug problem that was well underway in North America and, specifically, Canada. Part of the initiative included placing RCMP officers in New York, Los Angeles, and Miami, where they worked directly with the DEA and other law enforcement agencies to assist with thwarting the flow of illicit drugs. After WWII, the RCMP posted officers abroad under the auspices of the Foreign Liaison Directorate in HQ. With the Mulroney initiative, the three officers sent to the key American cities in the 1980s were absorbed and brought under the same command.

Rod Stamler was the decision-maker, selecting who would fill the three spots, and I got the nod for Miami. I was a known product, in the right place at the right time, and I had the prerequisite law enforcement experience, having worked many years on drug sections in British Columbia. I also had one other advantage: I was single with no dependents. Posting a person abroad is an expensive venture, with the added costs of a spouse, children, housing, private education, and travel. The whole show can become very costly.

Sending me to Miami was pretty straightforward. I finished up at HQ, flew to Miami, where a car and condominium were rented, and within a few days I was working. The drug enforcement directorate did not really have adequate funding or infrastructure in place for this type of move, and installing me quickly was simple—and cheap.

At this stage of my working life, I was thinking more strategically about what I wanted to do post-RCMP. It was now clear to me that advancing through the ranks in the RCMP was not something I was particularly interested in, so I started thinking about what was needed to be successful in the private sector. I had joined the RCMP as a young man, nineteen years old, and my formal education was minimal. While in Ottawa, I obtained a teacher's certificate from Algonquin College, which developed my presentation skills. This was helpful for my police duties, and later when I moved to the private sector, it augmented my business development efforts. I had also started going to night school in Vancouver in 1982, taking business classes, and continued at the University of Ottawa, work permitting. Prior to arriving in Miami, I had determined that Barry University, a private Catholic institution, had a strong program pitched toward mature students. Pursuing my degree at Barry University turned out to be absolutely the right move, albeit a long, arduous road to completing my studies prior to leaving Miami in 1992. Most of the courses completed, twenty-three in total, were business and accounting oriented, which helped set me up for opportunities after my RCMP career.

I arrived in Miami in April 1982 as the first full-time foreign liaison officer for the region. The Germans, British, French, and Italians subsequently assigned law enforcement people to Miami after my arrival. Miami had long been a pivotal hub for the smuggling of contraband, primarily cocaine, between South America and the rest of the world. It was also a financial center, and some of the banks were busy laundering the illicit funds generated from the sale of drugs. The cocaine cowboy days of taking bags of cash into banks had faded, but only by a couple of years. Miami has a large Latino population, and there were strong connections to source countries such as Colombia. Pablo Escobar was in his prime when I arrived, and large quantities of cocaine and marijuana were being moved via air and sea through the region to feed the American markets along with the demand coming from Canada and Europe.

With minimal guidance from management as to how things should be done prior to my arrival in Miami, I was left to figure it out on my own. As it turned out, this hands-off approach worked well for me.

CHAPTER FOUR
DEVELOPING THE NETWORK &
AVOIDING THE PITFALLS

- Do not ignore the red flags.
- Human sources are a critical element of effective law enforcement; developing rapport and trust is essential.
- Figure out who in law enforcement is actually making cases, and leverage that knowledge.

My new life in Miami was a significant change from my days in Ottawa. Of course, there was the polar opposite climate that inspired my newly discovered interests in tennis and scuba diving. I pursued both sports passionately and that, along with night school, easily filled my time off. Living in a government-subsidized, high-end condominium on Key Biscayne was pretty special: Key Biscayne is an island community in the greater Miami area, joined to the mainland by the Rickenbacker Bridge and Causeway.

I was dropped into a situation where there was no RCMP predecessor to show me the ropes, and the international law enforcement community had yet to arrive. I had to start figuring out how things worked, and specifically how to make cases. I did know there were always going to be requests and cases coming out of Canada, but I was largely alone at first to forge a path for myself in a new environment. Drug trafficking was synonymous with Miami, a city where people connected, trans-shipped, laundered money, and staged their illegal activities in southern Florida. I was confident this work would materialize, and it did, by the boatload.

Because I was the first permanent foreign law enforcement officer to be located in Miami, my main objective was to make my presence known. The American federal law enforcement agencies such as the FBI and DEA had their own people posted in Canada and would not necessarily need to engage me when Canadians came onto their radar. But the local and state departments did not have the luxury of having their own people working from the American embassy in Ottawa. I would network with people at conferences, meetings, drinking establishments, and other venues. This would spread the word that I was in Miami and a good source for their investigative objectives. This was in the pre-internet and pre-email age when meeting people and "pressing the flesh" was imperative.

During my posting in Miami, I lived in a condominium on Key Biscayne, an island community in the greater Miami area, studying and pursuing scuba diving and tennis in my time off.

I knew from my time working on the Vancouver Drug Section between 1978–83 that approximately 25 percent of investigators were pivotal in making cases. This is not to say that others were not working—they were—but most of the cases were being generated by the 25 percent at the forefront of the investigations. I assumed it would not be much different in Miami, and I wanted to figure out who these people were so I could be close to the action—hopefully some Canadian action. My path was slightly diverted by an introduction to someone outside of the law enforcement community on my arrival.

Shortly after arriving in Miami, I was introduced to a prominent Miami immigration attorney. He said he was formerly a state prosecutor in the New York area, though I never confirmed his claim. The introduction was done through the Canadian Immigration and Citizenship (CIC) representative working out of the Canadian Consulate in Atlanta. The attorney was very friendly and inclusive, introducing me to several United States Immigration & Naturalization Services (USINS) agents, whom he described as the "A" team. The "A" team was made up exclusively of USINS agents, eight people in total. He generously included me as part of this team.

The first couple of encounters were at the City Club, an up-market business club located on Biscayne Boulevard in Miami proper. It was not typically a place where law enforcement people hung out as its membership was above our pay grade. The attorney generously picked up the tab for the group on the two occasions when I joined him and the others. He subsequently started offering me tickets to professional and college sporting events. The offers came frequently.

I chose to stay away from the "A" team for a couple of reasons: first, I was not in Miami to do immigration work. (Maybe if a case fell into my lap, but it certainly was not a priority.) Second, I did not feel comfortable with this attorney's overtures. He seemed to exude a sleazy demeanor that I didn't like. I was also privy to some documents seized from a Colombian drug trafficker, and his phone book included the attorney's contact details. That was one red flag too many.

Fast forward to 1992, when shortly after arriving in London, an RCMP immigration investigator from Ottawa contacted me and disclosed he was involved in a joint investigation in Miami involving a person of interest with the attorney's name. I did not get any details on the investigation other than that USINS agents had been compromised along with a CIC person. Fortunately, I had no association with the attorney and the "A" team other than in my first year in Miami. The investigator asked me about the gratuities offered. My recollection was that I had accepted event tickets twice and had been offered them at least twenty times. My memory of things was consistent with what my buddy, Tom, had recorded in a ledger that he maintained. I was never contacted on this matter again, but it certainly was a huge reminder: do not ignore the red flags.

My geographical area of responsibility was the southeastern United States. For the most part, the cases were concentrated in Dade and Broward Counties where Miami and Fort Lauderdale are located, but other cases originated along the coastal areas of the Gulf of Mexico. There are miles of coastline along the gulf, and it was a straight shot to the USA for vessels from many locations in Mexico, the Caribbean, and even Colombia.

One typical smuggling case originated out of the Sarasota area on the Florida Gulf Coast. The FBI was working a joint case with local authorities. The main targets of the investigation were from Quebec—specifically the Eastern Townships area that is a couple of hours' drive east of Montreal. The contraband was being smuggled by vessel from Jamaica to the Florida coast, where it was to be off-loaded and eventually taken via land transportation to the New York State–Quebec border and on into Canada. I was asked to assist with getting the RCMP involved, helping identify targets, and generally coordinating the efforts of the Sarasota law enforcement initiative. As it turned out, the Canadian crime group demonstrated a level of sophistication, and their illegal activities had been going on for some time. The targets owned property that was located on the USA–Canadian border, and a local ski hill had been purchased in an effort to launder illicit revenues. It was a successful case, and I enjoyed working with the Sarasota crew.

WORKING WITH INFORMANTS

Law enforcement in the USA was different from what I was accustomed to. The use of cooperating informants (CI) was the norm for the Drug

Enforcement Administration (DEA) in Miami. I had worked with criminals who cooperated, but in Canada, it was considerably more difficult to get people to work with us because of much lighter sentencing guidelines compared with those meted out in the USA. If you are caught up in an investigation in the USA involving large amounts of contraband, it is very likely you could spend twenty-plus years, or even longer, in jail if convicted. The fear of spending such a long stretch of time in an American federal penitentiary was a big incentive for arrested people to strike a deal with the investigators. As a result of this fear, some Canadians who got "banged up" started to cooperate.

To secure a conviction in Canada, more involved investigations are required, and everything needs to be corroborated. Consequently, a typical case might start with an informant providing details about a smuggling venture, and then as the case moved along there would be phone taps, considerable surveillance, and police officers working in an undercover capacity. Conversely, in a DEA case, the CI would be set up to participate in a smuggling venture. This could be a pilot, for instance, who would report back to his handlers advising them when and where things were happening. Very seldom would phones be tapped.

Normally, Canadian smugglers would avoid entering an American jurisdiction for the obvious reason that there were serious consequences for smuggling illegal drugs. Because the USA lies between Canada and Latin America (LATAM), where much contraband originates from, efforts are made to skirt the USA via the Caribbean. In one case, a plane carrying contraband flew right into a hornet's nest, landing stateside, and suggesting that the pilot was most likely cooperating with authorities.

In May 1990, an agent from the Fort Lauderdale DEA office contacted me to advise that a load of contraband would soon be arriving in Florida from Colombia. It was to arrive on a DC-4, a cargo plane that is considered a workhorse by smugglers. Two Canadians would be on board the aircraft with the transported contraband. The plane was destined for Canada but stopping in Florida to refuel. In this particular case, there is no fear of retaliation by those involved because it occurred thirty years ago. Nevertheless, I've used pseudonyms in recounting the events.

In June 1990, the DC-4 arrived in the Miami area loaded with contraband, and as reported, two Canadians were onboard. I first met the two

Canadians at the Dade County lock-up and spoke with them individually after their arrest. Their contention was they had no intention of bringing contraband into the USA, and with the ultimate destination being Canada, there was no contravention of American laws. I patiently explained to both of them individually that there was little chance of the courts accepting this defense. I advised them to discuss their predicaments with legal counsel and then I would return for further dialogue. One of them got what I was after immediately, but the other was a bit slower to figure things out. The DEA agent who brought me in on the case had bigger fish to fry, and I was now handling the two Canadians myself. The one CI, whom I'll call Perry, had some good information I could act on.

I developed a rapport with Perry and made regular visits to the lock-up. I also simultaneously started to ingratiate myself with Perry's legal counsel. The legal counsel was very experienced with this type of scenario and encouraged Perry to work with me. Things went well.

A CI is given a certain length of time to work with law enforcement before sentencing, and it is during this window that cases need to progress. It was more challenging for Perry and me, because he was in custody and not getting out on bail, which would have made it easier to talk with him. However, prior to getting on the plane to Florida, he had been speaking with a crew from the Vancouver area who was in the process of arranging to smuggle a boatload of marijuana from Colombia to Canada, long before locally grown marijuana took over the market. I gathered as much information as possible and then began communicating with some of my former colleagues in Vancouver.

My inquiries were timely: an investigation was underway involving a West Coast crew who were in the throes of smuggling a boatload of marijuana and cocaine from Colombia to British Columbia. The information I was able to provide filled many of the gaps in the case for the investigators in British Columbia. The information provided by Perry exposed those who were providing the product, how it was to be transported, and, most importantly, the timing of the shipment. To further advance the project, two of the primary RCMP investigators flew down to Miami, where Perry's debriefing continued, and affidavits were prepared to support phone intercepts back in Canada.

The Vancouver investigation moved along smoothly for several weeks, and the net widened to include phone intercepts on targets located in Montreal, as well as Victoria. It is normal for a large-scale investigation to expand as the inflow of intelligence and evidence occurs. In this particular case, pay phones were being used extensively. Mobile phones were not commonly in use in the early nineties, and there certainly wasn't instant messaging. (Satellite phones were only used when on the ocean or in remote areas.) It was the age of old-fashioned, copper-wired landlines. Pay phones were used extensively by smugglers to evade surveillance as they facilitated more elusive communication. However, determined investigators were able to get court authority to intercept pay phone calls, with the only caveat that physical surveillance of the subject making the call was necessary for the taped communication to be permitted as evidence. In this particular project, there were two main targets, Kurt Nichols and Lance Robson, who arranged the transportation of the contraband. Thirty pay phones in the vicinity of their residences were hooked up. Nichols' home phone was also being monitored, and he would tell his co-conspirators to call him at the "office"—code for his favorite pay phone at a White Spot restaurant in central Vancouver.

On one occasion, a call was intercepted in the monitoring room on a Sunday, and inflections in the voices of the subjects suggested that the call was important. Nichols told the other party to call him at the office in one hour. It was a Sunday, and there was no surveillance team available to get into a position to observe the pay phone. In desperation, an investigator who lived near the restaurant scrambled to get into position and ordered a coffee. No sooner had he arrived, than Nichols showed up and the pay phone rang. On the call, Nichols was instructed to travel to Curaçao, an island country in the southern Caribbean, where he was to meet the people who would be bringing a load to Canada. This was a major breakthrough for the investigators. Nichols was receiving instructions from the money man in Montreal, Kalev Amon.

An investigator traveled to Curaçao prior to Nichols doing so, arriving where the local authorities had been engaged to assist with covering the anticipated meetings. Nichols rented a hotel room where he met a Colombian who shared information on how the "mother ship" and the off-load vessels and their crews were to communicate. Channels, code names, timelines, and expectations were discussed. The conversations in the room were being monitored via a listening device, which was helpful, but the subjects were using "Moscow Rules." This refers to a method of communication involving the writing of notes on paper without any spoken dialogue. The paper is burned when the meeting is completed. The smugglers did everything right, other than burning their notes; instead, they intended to flush them down the toilet. Nichols left the room after the meeting, and when the investigators later looked in the toilet, there were the torn-up paper scraps floating in the bowl. Luckily, they were able to piece the scraps back together and read what had been written down. Significant information was gleaned from the paper fragments, including radio channels and the codes that were to be used when communicating between the mother ship and the off-load boats. This was extremely fortunate; the investigators were slowly moving into a position of control.

BIG PROBLEMS

There is an old saying in law enforcement: "No cases, no problems; little cases, little problems; big cases, big problems." This project was moving along exceptionally well, but it was a big case. The vessel transporting the contraband would be coming up the western seaboard of the USA and, even though it would most likely remain in international waters for the voyage, American authorities were advised of the investigation. The plan was to monitor movement of the mother ship and allow it to reach its final destination. As the mother ship was making its way northwest of California, a U.S. Navy vessel began tracking it and fired some flares over the mother ship. This caused some consternation for the smugglers, and during nightfall, the load was dumped into the ocean. The ship also developed some mechanical issues and eventually landed at Half Moon Bay in California. It was a disappointing ending to an otherwise stellar investigation. There were conspiracy prosecutions in Vancouver that resulted in some convictions, but the many smugglers that would have been captured in the net at the takedown stage caught a huge break. It was never confirmed, but strongly believed, that the naval vessel, for some unknown reason, was sent out to harass the mother ship.

I continued to work with Perry with some success; he was eventually sentenced, albeit at a much-reduced term. It was not my last encounter with Perry; he will feature again later in the book.

DRUG TIES TO THE MOB & INSIDE CORRUPTION

Another source of information came by way of a German liaison officer (LO) with whom I had a good relationship. The German LO, Horst Kalish, was working with a source who was a mercenary operator. He had not been busted for many crimes, but rather worked cases with law enforcement for monetary gain. I will refer to him as Wolfgang.

While in Bolivia, Wolfgang had met a Canadian from Quebec who appeared to be well connected in the crime world. With the information provided by Wolfgang, and with assistance from the RCMP in Montreal, we were able to determine the identity of the person who turned out to be a lieutenant in the Rizzuto crime family. (The Rizzuto crime family is featured in a book, written by Lee Lamothe and Adrian Humphreys, called *The Sixth Family*, see Further Reading). The information provided by Wolfgang was high grade and piqued the interest of the RCMP in Montreal.

As the investigation progressed, Yves Duguay from the Montreal drug squad traveled to Miami, where the terms of Wolfgang's cooperation were documented, and a game plan was hatched. I was Wolfgang's handler; Duguay returned to Montreal, where he commenced the investigation into members of the Rizzuto organization.

Wolfgang massaged his relationship with the Rizzuto lieutenant to a point where he was asked to oversee a shipment of cocaine destined for Montreal. The load would trans-ship in Miami with the blessings of the DEA, and then a controlled delivery would be completed to its final destination. Everything was moving along well until I received a panicked call from Wolfgang, who was told that he was no longer trusted by the Bolivian source of the cocaine. The Rizzuto family had learned that a German national who went by the name of Wolfgang was working with law enforcement. The investigation was aborted immediately, and Wolfgang eventually made his way back to Miami in one piece.

When working in any country, but especially LATAM countries, one is always cautious not to compromise an investigation. The RCMP Liaison Officer from Lima who covered Bolivia had shared some information with the local authorities, but certainly not the identity of the cooperating source. My first intuition was that the investigation had been compromised in Bolivia; I surmised that somehow a corrupt law enforcement person had figured out the game plan and tipped off the cocaine source. I shared my thoughts with Duguay, and I will never forget his response: "I am not so sure the leak might not have been in Montreal." Duguay was in fact correct in his assessment.

Unbeknownst to me when I arrived in Miami, there was serious concern in Montreal about investigations not reaching their fruition because of information leaks. In the coming months, the officer-in-charge of the Montreal Drug Section, Inspector Claude Savoie, came under investigation. He was the top person on the section, and sadly before the investigation was concluded he took his own life by shooting himself in the head with his service revolver at RCMP HQ in Ottawa. Savoie had been transferred to Ottawa because of disquiet about his integrity.

During the same time period, a prominent criminal defense lawyer, Sidney Leithman, was active in providing services to Italian organized crime figures and other banditos in Montreal. There were strong indicators that while Savoie was in charge of the Montreal Drug Section, he had been compromised by Leithman, consequently leaking details that affected several investigations. The Canadian Broadcasting Corporation's investigative documentary unit, *The Fifth Estate,* produced an exposé on the Savoie story after he took his own life, which detailed the ex-officer's alleged involvement in Montreal's drug scene. The suspicions were never confirmed, due to the deaths of both Savoie and Leithman, but there was little doubt as to what had transpired.

Having credible sources is an essential element of effective contraband investigations. Reliable sources are difficult to cultivate, and when you are fortunate enough to work with one, there are many challenges with translating intelligence into prosecutable cases. First, you need to develop a rapport with the source that allows a bond to develop, leading to a trust factor. Once the trust factor has been established, then the challenge is to take strong intelligence and join the dots. In this particular case, I received strong intelligence regarding Montreal organized crime figures being met in Bolivia and discussing moving large amounts of cocaine to Canada. That is a good start, but then the work begins. The next step is to identify the targets and learn as much as possible about their illicit activities around their cocaine smuggling activities.

We were well on our way to moving the case forward where evidence could be gathered, and then everything was compromised. To have one of your own, like Savoie, switch sides, compromise an investigation, and put people at risk is hard to fathom. Savoie was originally from Willow Bunch, a small French-speaking community in Saskatchewan, with a population of a couple hundred people. Not much different from my own roots growing up in the hamlet of Druid, Saskatchewan. Looking back, I pondered what could have happened along the way to cause this kind of betrayal.

We were fortunate that no one was harmed due to the information leak, but it was tremendously frustrating, given that we were on the path to executing arrests of high-level smugglers.

CHAPTER FIVE
PRESIDENTS & DESPERADOS

- Extradition, American-style.
- Life on the island, a significant shift from my Canadian lifestyle.
- Getting a glimpse of Pablo Escobar's cartel.

Key Biscayne is a piece of paradise. It lies directly east of Miami and is part of the chain of islands that wind southwest into the Gulf of Mexico and end at Key West. Key Biscayne is not connected to the other islands via a bridge, but it is connected to the mainland via the Rickenbacker Causeway. The island is a ten-minute drive from the mainland, with a population of approximately ten thousand. It has beautiful beaches, a scuba diving center, and features the Crandon Park Tennis Center. The tennis center hosts the Sony Open that is the top-rated professional tournament after the four grand slam tournaments. During my time in Miami, playing and watching tennis became a big part of my life, and living near the tennis center was a real bonus. When the tournament—called the Lipton Open in the nineties—was happening, tickets were readily available during the first week. I would walk down the beach to the center, where I watched many greats of the day play, including Becker, Graff, Sampras, Sabatini, and Pierce.

Mary Pierce lived in the complex where I resided, and Gabriela Sabatini, an Argentinian, lived on the island as well. There were many high-net-worth Latinos living on Key Biscayne, some of whom had acquired their wealth through non-conventional methods.

Prior to my arrival, Richard Nixon had a secondary home on the island, and some of the old-timers spoke of when he would frequent the local establishments. His home was purchased by a Colombian named Roberto Striedinger, who built a palatial home on the property before my arrival. Striedinger acquired the seaside property for $5 million. Interestingly, I happened to cross paths with Striedinger during my time living on Key Biscayne.

In late 1988, a Canadian national by the name of Doug Jaworski approached the RCMP in Toronto with some interesting information. Revealing Jaworski's identity here is no longer a concern because he eventually testified, went into witness relocation, and featured in the book *The Big Sting*, written by Peter Edwards, a Toronto journalist (see Further Reading). Jaworski was an accomplished pilot and had become ensnarled in the Medellín Cartel because of his pilot skills and knowledge of aircraft. In 1986, his first encounter with the cartel was when he was tasked with flying a Gulfstream Commander Jetprop 1000 from Miami to Saint Martin in the Caribbean. This type of plane was ideal for long-haul shipments of cocaine. The plane was flown to Colombia, where it was put to work. Striedinger was the person whom Jaworski dealt with on one case where I was involved. Striedinger had previously been the "chief pilot" for the cartel, but refocused on other cartel business, including money laundering. Jaworski was enticed by the easy money he could make. However, the risks and consequences of his actions eventually weighed heavily on his mind. That was when he decided to switch sides.

I first became aware of Jaworski's cooperation when I received a call from Bob Lowe, a long-time drug squad officer in Toronto whom I had known since my undercover days there in 1976. Lowe provided some context to the project and indicated he would soon be traveling to Miami with Jaworski. On February 2, 1989, I flew to Toronto for meetings, and subsequent plans were hatched to move the investigation along.

Prior to Jaworski approaching the RCMP with his interesting story, he had been introduced to a Colombian national, one Alejandro Diego Vasquez Caycedo, who was one step away from Pablo Escobar. Caycedo was an urbane, intelligent operator who provided oversight for the transportation of cocaine from South America to the markets in North America and Europe. Originally, Caycedo wanted Jaworski to pilot planes laden with cocaine from clandestine airstrips in Colombia. Caycedo ultimately had Jaworski take on the role procuring aircraft and providing vital local knowledge about how to fly loads of cocaine into Canada. The first task was to locate and purchase a plane that could make the long, twelve-hour journey to circumvent American airspace by flying over the Atlantic and entering Canadian airspace in the Maritimes. Jaworski located a $4 million Astrajet for the purpose. His commission for that deal was $400 thousand, and this was just one of several plane transactions Jaworski capitalized on.

SWITCHING SIDES

Jaworski had, over a short period of time, acquired considerable wealth, and things were going smoothly until he received a visit from the Internal Revenue Service (IRS) in Fort Lauderdale. They were conducting a money laundering/tax evasion investigation that had identified Jaworski as a person of interest. He felt the heat and was looking for an exit from his life of crime with the cartel. Jaworski and Lowe arrived in Miami on March 30, and the first order of business was for Jaworski to meet Striedinger, who wanted to talk to Jaworski about some "business."

Jaworski had a boyish look, and was a soft-spoken and generally likable person in his mid-twenties. It became evident to me early on that he was an intelligent, smooth operator. On the day of their arrival, we traveled separately to Striedinger's home on Key Biscayne. After a brief stay, Jaworski was told to meet Striedinger at the Sheraton Hotel on Biscayne Boulevard. Because we had been put on short notice, the DEA was not brought in to assist, and Lowe and I surveilled the meeting in the restaurant where Striedinger described a money laundering scheme that involved Jaworski's knowledge of aircraft. With competing priorities, the opportunity to ensnare Striedinger in his scheme was not pursued. However, I did document the intelligence gathered and entered it into the DEA's system. The report and encounter with Striedinger resurfaced when Manuel Noriega was ultimately arrested in Panama by American authorities in January 1990.

Jaworski and his wife, Susan, lived in Fort Lauderdale. She was an attractive, successful, professional woman holding three degrees and a well-paying job. She had enjoyed the trappings of her husband's airplane business; their life was filled with all of the niceties money could buy. She was totally blindsided by what Jaworski had been up to. Many loose ends needed to be tied up before his cooperation with the police could be disclosed. His wife's situation had to be taken into account, along with that of his parents, who lived in the British Virgin Islands (BVIs). Unfortunately, while moving a plane to Colombia, Jaworski had taken a Medellín Cartel person to BVI where his parents were living. Everyone close to Jaworski was in for a rude awakening, and one of my tasks was to assist his wife Susan in making the transition to a new life.

The RCMP learned through Jaworski and other sources that planeloads of cocaine had been entering Quebec via American airspace and off-loading at Sorel Airport during the night hours when it was closed down. Someone at the airport had been compromised by the cartel and was facilitating the inbound flights from Colombia. On one occasion, fighter jets were scrambled in New England to follow the planes that came in unannounced at a low altitude. Unfortunately for law enforcement, no one was able to get into position to intercept the consignments, of which there were at least three.

Jaworski's highly placed cartel handler, Caycedo, was anxious to avoid American airspace and discussed sending flights out into the Atlantic and then doing a hard left west directly into Canada. Jaworski began to work on a plan, now with the assistance of his new police friends. Together they were able to identify an abandoned airstrip, Wayman Airfield, located close to Fredericton, New Brunswick, a short drive north of the Maine border. Jaworski also did his homework on logistical issues to evade being picked up by Canadian radar tracking incoming aircraft.

In late February, Jaworski made his final trip to Colombia, where he met with Caycedo and Fernando Augusto Mendoza-Jaramillo, also referred to as "Pinguino," who would co-pilot the Commander 980 that would take off from a remote airstrip in northern Colombia, laden with six hundred kilos (1,323 pounds) of cocaine. Pinguino was being paid $150 thousand per trip and had already taken three loads into Sorel, Quebec. Details and photographs were provided for Wayman Field, and financials were negotiated. Jaworski received instructions to take control of the load when it arrived and transport it to a secure location. After that task was completed, he would receive further instructions on the next moves. Jaworski would be paid $500 thousand for his efforts.

After returning to Canada, a cartel member from Miami, Diego Ganuza, arrived in Northern Maine with $430 thousand. The money was to pay for the airstrip and to cover other operating expenses. Subsequent to Ganuza arriving, Pinguino came up to New Brunswick to view the airstrip and discuss final details. His only concern was that there were tall trees at one end of the airstrip that could hinder the trajectory of the plane on approach to land. The airstrip had been out of service for a few years and not in ideal condition. There were discussions about removing the trees, but in the end a decision was made to forge forward without cutting them down.

On April 2, 1989 Jaworski received a call from Caydedo saying the plane had just left Colombia; barring any problems, it was scheduled to arrive at Wayman Field in eight hours. To accommodate the long flight and heavy load, extra fuel containers were cobbled together, potentially making the plane a flying time bomb. There were two pilots onboard.

Waiting in the weeds around Wayman Field were scores of Mounties, all ready to execute a successful investigation. The plan was to remove the pilots from the scene upon arrival and take them to a safe place where they could recuperate from the long, stress-filled flight. The cocaine would then be off-loaded and taken to the police lock-up, where it would remain until Jaworski received further instructions on where it was to be delivered. Up to this point, the RCMP did not consider the Colombians a big presence in central Canada, but they now knew differently. There were large consignments arriving, and other ongoing investigations identified three different cells operating in Montreal and Toronto. The cartel intentionally set up separate cells to avoid the possibility of each being taken out simultaneously by law enforcement.

TOUCHDOWN & TAKEDOWN

On April 3 at daybreak, the Commander 980 approached the runway for a landing. Adding to the stress of the fuel-laden aircraft, the pilots were on high alert as they thought another plane in the area was following them. In fact, the plane was a civilian aircraft that just happened to be in the vicinity. The pilots came in a bit low on the approach and, sure enough, one of the trees at the edge of the airfield was clipped, causing snow to fall from the branches. The contact with the branch resulted in an over-correction by the pilot, and he hit the brakes early, spinning out at a ninety-degree angle. When the plane finally came to a stop, the pilots bailed out, exclaiming gas was slopping around in the plane. They feared the whole thing could go up in flames. The pilots were picked up by two undercover operators, one a Spanish speaker, and were hurried out of the area. Then the other officers came out of the weeds and commenced off-loading the cargo and securing the aircraft. So far, so good.

The pilots were escorted out of the area where they laid low, waiting for the plane to be prepared for the flight back to Colombia. In the meantime, arrangements were being made to execute the controlled delivery of the cocaine to the Colombian cell in Montreal. Controlled deliveries can be challenging to execute properly; thus elaborate plans were made to enhance the chances of a successful outcome. Over one hundred officers were used to make the delivery. The first step was to substitute the drugs for sugar and to install listening devices. With sugar substituted for the contraband and loaded into a rented van, the vehicle was turned over to one of the Colombians on Drummond Street in downtown Montreal. It was then driven to a townhouse in Little Burgundy southwest of downtown. The team moved into the area, waiting and listening. After a short time, it became obvious the packages were being opened, and the officers then swarmed the residence, arresting everyone without any incident.

THE TRIAL

There are many other aspects to this investigation that cannot be elaborated on, including a failed attempt to break the Colombians out of jail in New Brunswick where the importation trial took place. The Colombians are known to use extreme violence to obtain their objectives, and being in Canada did not alter their way of operating. One example of how the criminal element can behave in Colombia was the guerrilla siege of the Palace of

Justice in Bogotá on November 6, 1985, when twenty-five supreme court justices were killed. Security was a serious consideration when the trials were taking place. There are international standards set for security, and the highest level for security is rated at seven; only people such as the Pope and the American president are provided with a level seven security rating. The trial and Jaworski himself were protected with a level 6.5 security level.

The main trial relating to the controlled delivery took place in Montreal, and this was where Jaworski's credibility and ability to testify were put to the test. The Colombians engaged someone whom they considered the best criminal defense lawyer in Montreal. Syd Leithman had a well-known reputation for being ruthless with the questioning while not being overly concerned about following generally accepted protocols for an officer of the court. It is rumored he received a $1 million retainer for his work, but it was unclear as to what his true remuneration was.

Jaworski did a commendable job of presenting his evidence, and the RCMP presented a watertight case. There was a 100 percent conviction result, which was followed up with some hefty sentences, at least by Canadian standards, which range around the twenty-year imprisonment mark. This was a major setback for the Colombian cartel in Canada, which was seriously annoyed by Leithman's performance, or lack thereof.

A DEADLY MESSAGE

On May 13, 1991 at 6:48 a.m., Leithman was minutes away from his home in Mount Royal, Montreal on his way to the office. He was riding alone in his black Saab convertible, and when Leithman was stopped at a red light, a man emerged from a phone booth and opened fire with a .45 automatic pistol. Leithman, the man who had himself ridiculed the tight courtroom security during his clients' trials, was killed instantly. As a final, apparently anti-Semitic flourish, a bag of smoked meat was tossed onto the body.

There is an old saying: "If you fly with the crows, expect to get some buckshot."

THE PANAMANIAN CONNECTION

Meanwhile, back in Miami, new things were happening involving Panama. Manuel Noriega had been a thorn in the American government's side for some time. He started out as an ally, cooperating with intelligence agencies and doing what was expected of a puppet leader. But then he started going off script, getting into bed with the Medellín Cartel while assisting with the movement of cocaine into the USA via Panama. This was a big mistake for which he paid a dear price.

In 1988, Noriega was indicted in Miami by Dick Gregorie, an Assistant U.S. Attorney whom I had met on different occasions. There was a famous Miami establishment called "Tobacco Road" that law enforcement and attorneys would frequent, especially on Fridays, at the end of the workweek. Tobacco Road was touted as Miami's oldest bar, having survived land booms, Prohibition, the Great Depression, and deadly hurricanes. It championed local musicians, primarily jazz performers, and, weather permitting, most patrons hung out in the back patio area. It was a fun place to spend a few hours to talk about the ones you caught and the ones that got away. During my visits to the bar, I was told more than once by Gregorie that he had indicted Noriega, and he predicted that justice would prevail for his drug-related activities. It certainly did, commencing with the invasion of Panama by the American military on December 20, 1989 and concluding with Noriega being treated to a one-way flight to Miami where he stood trial for cocaine importation. This is extradition, USA style.

The now-defunct bar Tobacco Road in the Brickell area of downtown Miami where law enforcement and attorneys would unwind, especially on Fridays at the end of the workweek. *(CC by Marc Averette)*

Global attention to the case put pressure on the DEA to deliver a strong prosecution. Tom Raffanello was assigned as the lead agent to prepare the case and gather the evidence. I had worked different cases with Raffanello, and he and his unit were an excellent choice for what lay ahead.

As mentioned previously, the DEA relied heavily on cooperating informants to assist with the prosecutions. Noriega operated from Panama behind the scenes, providing support and access to the cartels that were moving the drugs north. There was an urgent need to find people who would testify about their dealings with the rogue leader. That is when Roberto Striedinger came back onto the radar. In doing his research, agent Len Athas located the report submitted by me, detailing the restaurant meeting between Striedinger and Jaworski in March 1989 that was covered by Bob Lowe and myself. Other than Lowe and myself, no one had actually eyeballed Striedinger.

In early 1990, I was asked to assist with identifying Striedinger while assisting with gathering more information on his activities. Conveniently, Striedinger had the old Nixon home up for sale. I arranged through the listing agent to have a tour of the house. When speaking with the real estate agent, I was able to determine that Striedinger was living at the house. This was also confirmed by observations I made. Although not present at the time, the realtor stated Striedinger was most likely out for a boat ride with out-of-town visitors. This information was passed on to Athas, and later that day I was asked to travel to a marina where a boat with four people on it was under surveillance. I approached the boat at dock, where I engaged in a conversation with the person whom I believed was Striedinger. I could not be 100 percent certain, because he now sported a beard. My one encounter had been from the other side of a restaurant some time before. I shared my thoughts with Athas, and that was good enough for him. Striedinger was arrested on an outstanding warrant, and predictably, he became one of the star witnesses that put the nail in Noriega's coffin. Striedinger was the key transportation coordinator for the cartel and had met with Noriega several times to arrange the transshipment of drugs to the US. Striedinger never did get to benefit from the sale of his palatial house: its new owner was now the American government.

****

By now it was 1992, and I had ended four-plus years in Miami. My time in Miami had been adventurous and productive. At any one time I would have up to twenty files on the go, some of which would be standard inquiries to locate a person or conduct background inquiries. Plus, there were other, more involved matters, where Canadians were in Miami intending to further their efforts to smuggle drugs or launder money. These types of files would often involve organizing surveillances, dealing with informants, and coordinating with investigators. I thrived on this kind of work.

Initially, I was told by the director of foreign services that I would be finishing up in July and heading back to Canada. That actually suited me fine, but then came an unexpected opportunity. For reasons not clear to me, I was offered a cross-posting to London, which I eagerly accepted, and in late July I was off. I left town just in time. Three weeks after my departure Hurricane Andrew landed in South Florida, and Key Biscayne took the brunt. Not one tree was left standing on the island when it was all over.

CHAPTER SIX
LONDON & BEYOND

- Expanding the network to another level.
- Being present while history is taking place.
- Those ever-important note taking habits.

I was able to complete my business degree in June 1992, a month before the end of my stint in Miami, and I was in the process of putting my application package together to obtain accreditation with the Association of Certified Fraud Examiners. I was confident both would go a long way in improving my profile and skills for future opportunities.

As it turned out, two opportunities unexpectedly presented themselves. The first was by way of my former mentor, Rod Stamler. Stamler was now heading up Forensic Investigative Associates (FIA) in Toronto, and he flew me to Toronto where we discussed a position that the firm was offering. The offer was enticing, but I felt it was a bit premature to leave the RCMP as I had just arrived in London, which, in itself, had the potential to be a good gig for me.

Another offer came up in 1994 from Norman Inkster. Inkster was retiring as the commissioner of the RCMP and also held the position as president of Interpol. He had just announced his retirement after accepting a job with the global accounting and consulting firm KPMG, and he was recruiting to build an investigative team. I attended an Interpol meeting in Rome where Inkster made a pitch for me to work for him at KPMG. Again, enticing, but the timing was a bit off. Inkster went on to hire several RCMP officers, including Don Svenson, Chris Mathers, and Doug Nash, which turned out to be a successful formula.

Being a liaison officer in London was an entirely different scene from what I had just left. I was now working out of Canada's second-largest foreign mission, the Canadian High Commission, and entrenched within the diplomatic milieu. Unlike Miami, numerous countries had law enforcement people assigned to London; the USA alone had approximately fifteen people from different federal agencies. I now had a boss, Bob Paradis, who had been in London for five years prior to my arrival, and our geographical area of responsibility included the UK, Ireland, and the Nordic countries.

Historically, the RCMP have had people posted permanently abroad, since post-WWII when they assisted with the vetting of displaced people throughout Europe. The RCMP had a unit—the Security Service Section—that was tasked with national security issues. In the early days, most people going to foreign postings came from that side of the force, rather than the criminal-investigations side. This was beginning to change upon my arrival in 1992, and I was considered part of a new breed that had been honed on chasing criminals, rather than spies. In 1984, the Canadian Security Intelligence Service (CSIS) was created, and national security was removed from the RCMP's mandate.

There were plenty of opportunities for good work out of the London office. I first focused my attention on the Isle of Man and Channels Islands, both offshore tax havens that attract a nefarious element, money launderers, and fraudsters. The G7 countries had just created the Financial Action Task Force (FATF) with a mandate to coordinate the curbing of money laundering. These were heady days for law enforcement people working in this sector. Also, London being a global financial center meant there was a large law enforcement presence pursuing high-level fraudsters who were using the system to exploit clever schemes that were being hatched continually. As we know, the UK colonized a large part of the world, and consequently, goods and people coming from all directions came through Heathrow airport and elsewhere en route to their destinations. Courier and contraband interceptions at these hubs were a regular occurrence.

The civil strife in Northern Ireland was at its apex as well. CSIS coordinated on the national security issues, but many things, such as the procurement of arms, flowed over to the criminal side. I made numerous trips to Belfast, where personal security concerns were tantamount. The Irish Republican Army (IRA) was considered the most organized and effective terrorist group in the world at the time. It would successfully target high-profile individuals like Lord Mountbatten, along with any other government officials who represented authority and Britain. This included police officers. The Royal Ulster Constabulary (RUC) was the only law enforcement body in Northern Ireland, and over the years, many officers were murdered simply because they were considered part of the British-backed establishment. Lord Mountbatten was a member of the British royal family and was a distinguished naval officer. In August 1979, he was assassinated with members of his family when the pleasure craft he was on in the Irish Sea was destroyed by a bomb.

When I was in Belfast, strict security protocols were followed, and I was always relieved when I left the region for the safety of London. The hatred between Catholics and Protestants in Northern Ireland was a foreign concept to me, and when in Northern Ireland, it was foolish to disclose one's religion for fear of retribution. In the RCMP, for the most part, no one knew or cared about your religious affinity.

In the early 1990s, the world was witnessing exceptional changes in the global order. The Cold War was winding down, glasnost and perestroika were well underway, and these world events changed the focus for law enforcement. Directives from HQ to our London office indicated that we now had geographical responsibility for the Former Soviet Union (FSU). My boss, Bob Paradis, was near to finishing his time in London and with the RCMP. He had zero interest in going to the FSU; it was all mine.

WELCOME TO THE WILD EAST

I regarded the new directives as yet another opportunity, albeit a much different one from opening the Miami office. The FSU had eleven time zones and numerous satellite regions including Ukraine, the Baltics, and Central Asia. Again, as in Miami, there was no established path to follow, as I was the first RCMP officer to be assigned to cover this area. Only the Americans had started to make some in-roads with law enforcement. I was told that within one to two years, an RCMP person would be posted permanently to Moscow; in the meantime, it was to be covered from London. My hours in the sky ramped up significantly.

My trips to the Former Soviet Union during my time in London were many. On this particular trip, two Isle of Man investigators joined me. They are the only ones smiling directly behind me. I introduced them to some Russian contacts who assisted them on a money laundering investigation.

Russia in the early 1990s was referred to as the "Wild East." President Boris Yeltsin was ostensibly in charge, the oligarchs were siphoning off state assets, and thugs were running amuck. It was close to complete anarchy. When visiting Moscow, I normally stayed at the Radisson Hotel located on the Moscow River with close proximity to the embassies and government offices. Extortion was the order of the day, but the manager of the Radisson, a Canadian, would have no part of it. His resistance was met with violence: he was summarily executed 100 meters from work.

Another incident occurred in the hotel restaurant while patrons were seated for breakfast. Gunmen opened fire on a targeted person, killing him on the spot. Unfortunately for a British businessman seated close to the victim, he caught a bullet and expired as well. The old system of complete control had vanished, and the void was filled by opportunists of all stripes. As the old communist system imploded, any semblance of control broke down, and everything was for sale. Everything. Body parts, military equipment, information, and anything people could leverage into money so they could survive was bartered in some fashion. Apartments in Soviet times were owned by the state. With the changeover in regimes, the occupants were given title to their homes, and they became first-time property owners. Property prices in Moscow jumped very quickly in the 1990s, providing an opportunity for the unscrupulous, of which there were many. Many elderly people had no sense as to the market value of the asset they were living in, and they sold their newly acquired properties for well below market value, the buyers in turn making large sums of money from these transactions. Many years later, when I was working in the private sector, I was engaged to conduct due diligence on a wealthy Russian who had mastered the art of duping elderly people. He owned over fifty apartments in central Moscow. He had been a KGB officer earning $1,500 a month in the early 1990s.

THE LAND OF TRUSTING FOOLS

In 1993, the RCMP established the Eastern European Organized Crime Task Force (EEOCTF) in Toronto, and a newly appointed inspector, John Neilly, took command. There were some badass Russian criminals on the streets of Toronto committing crimes and causing consternation for law enforcement. These criminals were prone to violence, and there were occurrences where shootings happened on the street. For the most part, Russians were victimizing their compatriots, and many of the crimes had an aggressive element to them.

One of my early tasks was to establish contacts with law enforcement personnel in Moscow who could assist with mitigating the problems on Canada's streets and also assist with vetting visa applicants. The Russian criminal element in Toronto was obtaining visas from the Canadian Immigration and Citizenship (CIC) office at the Canadian embassy in Moscow.

My first stop was the Interpol office in Moscow, where I met with Yuri Melnikov, the person in charge. At first, Melnikov was not overly cooperative, stating that Interpol's mandate was for criminal matters only; visa vetting was not in his bailiwick. After much cajoling and some negotiating, we eventually came to a resolution. He agreed to provide criminal record checks on selected visa applicants, which was a good first step. One thing I learned early on was that the Russian criminal element had little respect for how Canada did things. They had terminology to describe our country. Translated into English it was "the land of the trusting fools."

The need to support CIC in the FSU continued for the entire four years I spent traveling there, but once the processes were shored up my concentration switched to focusing on more sophisticated criminal characters, two of which were Boris Birshtein and Dmitri Oligovich Iakoubovski.

Birshtein was born in Lithuania, before moving to Israel like many Jews from the FSU, and then to Toronto in 1982. He originally colluded with Leonid Brezhnev's Soviet government to set up joint ventures facilitating the movement of state assets into the western economies. This served as a way to get much-needed western currency into the flagging Soviet economy. As one would expect, there was considerable leakage making its way into the pockets of individuals.

A company called Seabeco was one entity established to help move funds from the west to the Soviet Union. Seabeco was registered in Switzerland (no surprise there) and by the early 1990s had eight hundred employees and gross revenues of $500 million per annum. The company established an office in Toronto through which it was selling Soviet commodities, chemicals, and fertilizers to western economies. One of my early tasks was to exchange and gather intelligence on Birshtein with the Russian authorities. He had become *persona non grata* with the Yeltsin regime, but trying to communicate with anyone in the convoluted Soviet government apparatus was like walking through a maze. Eventually, authorities were able to curtail

Birshtein's activities. He was excluded from entering the UK and other countries and relocated to Switzerland. He features extensively in *Kleptopia: How Dirty Money is Conquering the World*, a book written by British author Tom Burgis (see Further Reading). On page 316, there is a reference to Birshtein's son-in-law, Alex Shnaider, who invested in the Toronto Trump Tower, and elaborating on the relationship between Donald Trump and Shnaider (now one of Canada's wealthiest men).

THE RUSSIANS ARE COMING

It is uncanny how some Soviet nationals were able to transition from a communist system into being mega-wealthy in such a short period of time. Many of the original oligarchs eventually made their way to the UK, and *Londongrad,* a book written by Mark Hollingsworth and Stewart Lansley, provides an interesting overview of several different individual stories in that country (see Further Reading). In the early 1990s, *nouveau riche* Russians were also making their way into western countries, including Canada. They were masters at taking advantage of the vulnerable elite. Professionals, politicians, and other established people unwittingly gave certain Russians an entrée into mainstream society. The EEOCTF was developing intelligence in Toronto on who was being compromised. I am not at liberty to disclose names, but many of these people were well-known to the public at the time.

Interestingly, a personal friend of mine was victimized by a clever Russian who wanted to get established in New York City. My friend went to law school as a mature student at NYU and graduated near the top of his class in 1993. He was offered an attractive position with an established Manhattan law firm. Within months of starting with the firm, he called me from Heathrow. He was on his way home from Kazakhstan and was changing planes. He was returning from a business trip with two new clients. I remember thinking that they must be *really* good clients, especially for someone just getting started in the legal business. A few months later I was in New York where I learned my friend was no longer with the firm and now was out on his own. His wife told me one of the Russian clients he brought into the firm turned out to be a high-profile nefarious character who later featured in a

Washington Post article. The firm was embarrassed, and my friend was shown the door for introducing such a bad actor. How did he meet the Russian, I asked. Well, it turned out to be the old, classic method of compromising the vulnerable elite. The Russian went to the law school where he posted an advertisement soliciting legal counsel. My friend ended up being exactly what they were looking for: top of the class, mature, and soon to be destined to work with a prestigious Manhattan law firm.

Another interesting character who arrived in Toronto in 1992 was Dmitri Olegovich Iakoubovski, a twenty-nine-year-old former Soviet military officer who was living in a $5.3 million home on Toronto's tony Bridal Path. Iakoubovski was doing quite well, considering he began as a humble communist in the Soviet Union only a couple of years before arriving in Toronto. A *New York Times* article dated October 2, 1993, titled "Russians Are Coming, but for Money" expressed the following:

> Thanks to relatively loose entry policies, tens of thousands of Russians have settled in Canada in recent years. Many are Jews who sought refuge from oppression in the former Soviet Union. But now Toronto is feeling a new wave of Russian immigration: the wheeler-dealers. They are among the new economic immigrants and are young, aggressive, ambitious capitalists using Toronto as a base for deals with the mother country.

After New York, Toronto was receiving the second highest number of Russian émigrés.

Iakoubovski was investing much of his ill-gotten wealth in Canada and was jetting back to Moscow on a regular basis. One of his specialties was selling Russian state-owned antiquities. The EEOCTF was building a case on him, and I had developed some strong working relationships with law enforcement people in Moscow who seemed to share the same objectives as my colleagues. Iakoubovski and Bershtein were loyal to two different camps in Moscow and were at loggerheads on both sides of the Atlantic. They also had an ongoing legal dispute before the courts in Toronto. Iakoubovski is featured in *The Encyclopedia of Canadian Organized Crime: From Captain Kidd to Mom Boucher*, written by Peter Edwards (see Further Reading).

The objective of each investigation was to gather enough evidence to support criminal charges being brought against Iakoubovski. It was more likely this would be possible in Russia, given this was where most of the illicit activities were taking place. The two criminal justice systems are much different and made it challenging to exchange evidence between Canada and Russia, but nevertheless, that was what I was asked to assist with. In early 1994, the EEOCTF forwarded a comprehensive report covering much that was known about Iakoubovski's activities, and I was asked to pass it on to my contacts in Russia. The report had been translated into Russian by the RCMP in Toronto as a courtesy. I had been working closely with two officers from the Moscow *Ministerstvo Vnutrennikh Del* (MVD), now known as the Ministry of Internal Affairs of the Russian Federation (MIA), one of whom spoke English. He had provided a facsimile number and asked me to use it when sending documents. I sent through the report written in Russian, and within an hour the contact called me in a bit of a panic. I was told to send only reports in English going forward, and to call first to ensure he was standing by the facsimile machine to receive the incoming document. I understood his concern but did not give the matter much more thought.

On Saturday, March 13, 1994, I received a call from my boss, Bob Paradis, who wanted to meet to discuss something he had just learned from HQ in Ottawa. Apparently, there had been a compromise in Moscow involving matters I had been handling, and both of us were summoned to Ottawa for meetings on March 15. We headed across the Atlantic on the fourteenth.

Shortly after arriving at RCMP HQ on the Monday morning, it became evident I was the main focus of attention. Two things had occurred in recent weeks. First, the report I had sent to Moscow MVD had been found in Iakoubovski's possession when his luggage was searched at Montreal airport's border control. It was an exact copy of the report, page for page. Second, another one-page, handwritten report with telephone numbers on it had been given to CSIS in Moscow by a source. The suggestion was that I had been compromised in some fashion. The first matter of the facsimile copy was unfortunate but not unusual in the context of Russia, where everything was for sale. Apparently, a clerk read the report, saw an opportunity to make some money, and sold it to our target.

The second matter of the notes written in my own handwriting was a bit different. I readily acknowledged the one-page report was generated by me, and I explained that on February 16, I had visited the Moscow MVD HQ where I met with members of the Economic Crimes Unit. I had turned the document over and asked if they could obtain subscriber details for phone numbers listed on the piece of paper. In retrospect, this was perhaps a casual, unorthodox way of making this sort of request, but the matter being investigated had arrived on my desk from Canada just prior to my departure for Moscow, and there was not time to include the details in a formal report. The allegation was that someone had managed to get into my briefcase and remove the handwritten document without my knowledge as I quaffed vodka with the MVD officers.

One of the questions about the translated Iakoubovski report was: why would I hand over a document containing so much detail? People at HQ were suggesting that it was intended for my eyes only. This was complete nonsense, as I was asked to conduct an investigation in tandem with the MVD and directed to share the report with my contacts in Russia. My response to the matter was twofold: Making detailed notes was something I had been doing since my undercover days. I had made an entry after receiving instructions from a certain officer that the report was to be delivered to the Russians. And I made the point that if the report was translated into Russian, how could it be for "my eyes only," considering I could not read Russian. There wasn't any good reason that I could think of, and it seemed that neither could the wizards at HQ. We were just chasing our tails in this matter.

My reply to the question of the one-page, handwritten report was that I had indeed been drinking vodka with MVD officers, that it was not a regular occurrence but was sometimes customary when doing business with the Russians. I also advised the interviewers that when traveling into the FSU I took only reports that were to be shared with the Russian authorities, nothing more. Nor would I take a laptop, which could be compromised. It was my contention that whoever turned the document over to CSIS was simply trying to make a buck and tarnish my reputation. I don't think it was personal; it was just the way things were done in those days to pay the bills. I would be interested to know what CSIS paid for the worthless piece of paper turned over to them by their inside person.

After sitting around Ottawa for most of the week, Paradis and I climbed back on the jet and returned to London. It was business as usual.

There are many more stories from my travels to the FSU that could be told, including being under surveillance, being solicited by prostitutes (agents), and having my room bugged—all common practice, even to this day. I recall one such laughable event in Kiev. I had been there for a couple of days, and it became obvious that every move I made was being monitored. On my last day in Kiev, I was sitting in my hotel room, thinking about dinner and who would be watching me when I went to the restaurant downstairs. I suspected a surveillance team would be close by, and I guessed they might be one floor down. I guessed right. When I left the room, rather than waiting for the elevator, I went quickly to the stairs, descended one flight, and encountered three or four gentlemen whom I caught like deer in the headlights lounging in a foyer area.

****

One of the last RCMP investigations I undertook before leaving London involved another member of the international jet set. I was engaged in a matter involving Dodi Fayed, whom Princess Diana died with in a much-documented Paris car crash in 1997. Fayed's father, Mohamed Al-Fayed, was the owner of the luxury London department store, Harrods, and his head of security was John McNamara, a retired Scotland Yard officer. McNamara approached me at the Canadian High Commission, asking for assistance in dealing with an Egyptian national who was impersonating Fayed in Toronto and defrauding people. Fayed was in the film industry, and the impostor was pitching opportunities to invest in his film projects. It was a damage control exercise.

I got an investigator in Toronto to commence with some inquiries while McNamara and I scheduled a meeting with Fayed. We met him the first time in June in central London. It was an underwhelming experience. Fayed showed up an hour late for the meeting, and McNamara was fuming. Fayed seemed vacant and disengaged, and McNamara asked Fayed to meet us again in a couple of weeks with information that would assist in the investigation. Fayed showed up late again for the second meeting, and he hadn't done anything that was asked of him at the first meeting. McNamara was irritated even more, as Fayed had behaved like a self-indulgent son of a super-wealthy family.

In 1994, Paradis's replacement, Larry Comeau, arrived in London. Comeau shared the travel and FSU workload with me and relieved a lot of the stress related to the job. Iakoubovski was eventually incarcerated in Russia, where he served time just as my stint in London was winding down. The RCMP subsequently had some challenges finding another officer to take my place on the Moscow dossier, and after a couple of potential people did not work out, it was offered to me again. I had already been posted abroad for over nine years, and going to Moscow for four more years was not in the cards. Eventually an experienced liaison officer, Jim Bates, was selected to fill the post.

I was now looking over the fence and getting ready for a new career outside of the RCMP. I transferred in July 1997 to the Vancouver Drug Section, where I would head up a target team. I left London in late July for Vancouver, and on August 31 when I was watching the evening news I briefly revisited a moment from my former life in London: Fayed and Princess Diana had just crashed in a Paris tunnel.

CHAPTER SEVEN
THE BLUE DAWN INVESTIGATION

- Exiting the RCMP, and one last smuggling case.
- Realizing my interest in being a Mountie was dwindling fast.
- Execute, execute, execute.

During my time in London, I had kept in touch with Rod Stamler, and he suggested stopping in Toronto on the way to Vancouver where we could discuss possible opportunities. By the time I made the stop and met with Stamler and some of the Forensic Investigative Associates (FIA) team, things had changed. I did not realize it at the time, but Stamler was getting ready to wind down and move away from the hectic pace he had been setting for the last few decades. We discussed how I could work with FIA when I got set up in Vancouver, but there were no specifics. I was a bit disappointed after the meeting, but not deterred from the idea of working with FIA in some capacity.

I was put in charge of the Unit Two team on the Vancouver Drug Section on my return to Vancouver. Its mandate was to target maritime smuggling, but the team was in the doldrums, as not much had been going on for a while. The person in charge of the section was an experienced investigator who was fully committed to catching bad guys and not consumed with self-promotion. His name was Terry Towns. Towns was a pleasure to work with and a breath of fresh air compared to some of the not-so-motivated managers I had encountered in the past. He was a no-nonsense boss, and this was a good fit for me.

Through the years, there have been many maritime smuggling ventures investigated by the RCMP in British Columbia involving large vessels coming from source countries loaded with contraband. Vancouver Island and the Mainland have miles of remote coastline, making them ideal for smugglers to land and unload without detection. When I arrived on Unit Two, one such investigation was in its early stages. Brad Trainor had been communicating with the Drug Section in Yarmouth, Nova Scotia, where one Sandford "Sandy" Hately had come to their attention. Hately was known to the RCMP as he was a suspect in a 1984 hashish importation investigation where four tons of hash were smuggled into a location three hundred miles north of Vancouver. Due to a lack of evidence, Hately was not convicted. Hately had recently purchased an oceangoing vessel, the *Blue Dawn*, in New Brunswick and had moved it to Yarmouth, where it was getting refitted. The vessel was being equipped with extra fuel tanks and twelve watertight compartments. Hately was paying for the work in $15-thousand installments comprising twenty-dollar bills bundled in brown paper bags. Hately's explanation for the boat's refits was that he would be returning with the vessel to British Columbia via the Panama Canal and would engage in the business of refueling tuna fishing boats. No one believed the story.

ELECTRONIC TRACKERS

Later in the year, the vessel departed, unobserved. A lookout was posted, and a few weeks later the *Blue Dawn* was reported to be mid-Atlantic in the Azores. The next spotting was in Gibraltar, where Hately and the vessel remained for a period of time, with a subsequent sighting of the vessel in Crete. A plan was hatched to travel to Greece with the intent to install a tracking device in the vessel. Hately did not seem to be in any hurry, but he was being cautious; the vessel was never left vacant. Consequently, a plan needed to be devised that would get Hatley and the crew off the boat long enough to allow a tracking device to be planted. The Hellenic Coast Guard agreed to help and took Hately and his crew to the police office, where they were questioned about a murder that had happened in the marina. The guise worked, and the device was installed in January 1998. We were now in control and could monitor the movement of the vessel from a computer in Vancouver. We also determined that an individual by the name of Ronald Grant was crewing for Hately. Grant was known to authorities, having been convicted three times between 1974 and 1987 for different drug offenses.

Hately eventually left Crete, transiting through the Suez Canal with a stop in Djibouti. The vessel sat there for a number of weeks. We had other intelligence indicating that a load of hashish was going to be picked up in Pakistan, and we surmised that Hately and his crew were in a holding pattern, waiting to pick up the cargo.

A HOTEL A DAY KEEPS THE DOCTOR AWAY

As we monitored the movements of the *Blue Dawn*, the investigation continued in Canada. We determined that between June 3 and January 6, Hately had traveled to Toronto on ten different occasions and stayed at the Strathcona Hotel downtown. Most stays were for one day, and we surmised he was receiving further instructions and picking up money. Even after the vessel had been moved to the Mediterranean, he flew back on three more occasions.

It takes considerable experience and resources to orchestrate a smuggling venture such as the one we were investigating. We knew this was a sophisticated group; however, they were making some mistakes. Allowing Hately to travel under his true identity was mistake number one, as he was well-known to authorities. Using the same hotel consistently was mistake number two. There is an old saying among smugglers: "A hotel a day keeps the doctor away." The "doctor" in this case was the police. Constant change is always recommended to stay one step ahead of anyone who may be on your trail.

On January 5, 1998, Hately was back in the Vancouver area, where he was observed meeting with his brother Joel and other players. We did not have authority to intercept communications at this stage, but we suspected that this was an exchange of more information about communications and logistics. We started to focus on Joel Hately and others who were identified through surveillance.

On September 7, 1998, Joel Hately traveled to Amsterdam. On his arrival, we had one of our investigators waiting with a Dutch surveillance team coordinated by the local RCMP Liaison Officer. Joel Hately met James Fallen, another Canadian in Holland, and together they purchased radios that were transported to Thailand. The Vancouver investigator, Peter Lea, eventually moved to Thailand from Holland and continued to follow Fallen, who had the equipment. The RCMP Liaison Officer in Bangkok was now involved and assisting with the investigation.

Eventually the *Blue Dawn* left Djibouti, sailed into the Indian Ocean, past Pakistan, and down to the Straits of Malacca, and stopped in Phuket, Thailand. We were now playing the waiting game. The vessel remained under observation while moored in Phuket.

On September 11, 1998, the *Blue Dawn* backtracked eight hundred kilometers (five hundred miles) and stopped for six hours off the southern tip of India, where it remained dead in the water. *The Blue Dawn* then moved in an easterly direction back down the Straits of Malacca, traveling at an average speed of nine knots per hour, slower than it had been sailing before. We were convinced that the vessel had been loaded with contraband during its six-hour stop at sea. The vessel continued through the South China Sea and into the Pacific. At its speed of travel, the *Blue Dawn* was estimated to arrive off the coast of British Columbia on October 27, 1998. Back in Vancouver, we were preparing for the welcoming party.

We caught a break in our investigation when another ongoing inquiry on Vancouver Island came to our attention. The drug section in Nanaimo had developed a source who, a couple of years earlier, had assisted with a hash off-load at Fanny Bay on Vancouver Island. The importation had been organized by a crime group from central Canada, and it was in the throes of bringing in another boatload. The source identified two individuals named Ronald and Kenneth Thomson, along with Wolfgang Fitznar from the Vancouver Island's Duncan area, who were making arrangements for the arrival of a vessel loaded with hash. The Thomson brothers were well-known to authorities and had been facilitating off-loads for many years.

The two investigations were joined together through the surveillance of a person named Sylvie Goyer from Quebec. Goyer was staying in a boutique hotel in the West End of Vancouver. She became central to the Vancouver investigation, and she was under 24-7 surveillance. She was observed meeting Fitznar when they went for a walk in the park while they talked. This was standard operating procedure for smugglers.

Intercepting inbound vessels with contraband is a resource-intensive exercise. Drafted to assist were many agencies and their assets, including the Canadian Navy, American Coast Guard, American Customs, RCMP Marine-Air Sections, and dozens of law enforcement personnel. In total, approximately 150 people were involved in the intercept. A communications center was set up at the RCMP HQ in Vancouver, and for the last three months of the project we had two shifts working twelve hours a day, seven days a week. I was in charge of the day shift.

The last three months of my active RCMP service was an intense, seven-day-a-week marathon intercepting the *Blue Dawn*. It could not have been scripted better. I loved the "thrill of the hunt," and this was as good as it gets.

On one Sunday morning shortly after I arrived at the communications center, the surveillance teams reported that Goyer had just boarded a taxi with her bags, apparently checking out of her hotel, and she was on the move. The surveillance team followed her to Vancouver International Airport. We scrambled to get our people to the airport, as we wanted to be on board the same flight that she was presumably taking. Goyer entered the airport and went into the washroom.

After a short period of time, an observant surveillance person saw Goyer departing the washroom, but now wearing different clothing and a wig and sporting a new look. Goyer then left the airport and got into a taxi that we followed for approximately fifty kilometers (thirty miles) to New Westminster. There, she entered a Greyhound bus station, where she purchased a ticket and departed on an eastbound bus, exiting the bus another fifty kilometers (thirty miles) down the road at Langley. At the Langley bus station, Goyer put a bag in a locker and then entered another taxi heading back to Vancouver, eventually returning to the same hotel from which she had departed earlier in the day. A search warrant was obtained for the locker, and several mobile phones, numerous passports in different names, and a large wad of cash were found inside the bag placed in the locker. The purpose of Goyer's travel that day was a classic cleaning exercise to deposit items and cash for future use.

The *Blue Dawn* continued on its trans-Pacific passage with a trajectory that would land the vessel approximately halfway up the British Columbia coast. We had also determined that the Vancouver Island crew had engaged a local fisherman to meet with the *Blue Dawn*, transfer the cargo to his vessel, and bring it into Fanny Bay, where it then would be off-loaded and taken to a storage location.

Voyage of the Blue Dawn

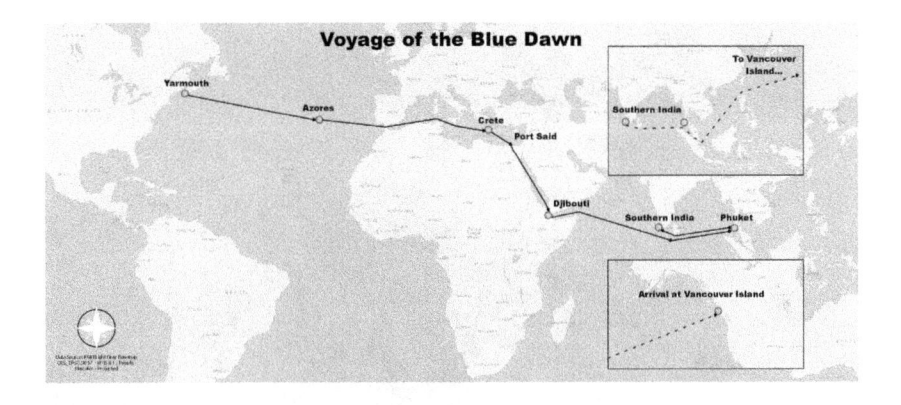

THE TAKEDOWN

The wrap-up of the investigation went down as planned. The local fisherman went out on his vessel, named the *Ansare II*, and met the *Blue Dawn*, which was waiting about 650 nautical miles west-northwest of Port Hardy, located on the northern end of Vancouver Island. The first transfer was made, and the skipper made his way back to the Fanny Bay area, where everyone waited for the cover of darkness to unload. When the off-load commenced, everyone sprang from their hiding places and swooped up the drugs and people. A U.S. Coast Guard and a Canadian Navy ship then steamed toward the *Blue Dawn*, which had ample time to dump some of the hash into the ocean. When the *Blue Dawn* was boarded, investigators found Sandy Hately and Ronald Grant, along with 2.5 tonnes (2.75 tons) of hash. Another 9.5 tonnes (10.5 tons) of hash were seized at Fanny Bay and, in total, fourteen people were arrested and charged. The takedown occurred on November 4, 1998.

The Blue Dawn investigation involved a crew of many officers working overtime. Pictured here is some of the Vancouver crew with me in the white coat and tie.

The long process of disclosure and preparing for trial began. It took several years before convictions were registered against all fourteen individuals. To the credit of the smuggling organization, it bankrolled the considerable defense costs for the smugglers. Every possible aspect of the evidence entered was fought to the bitter end, including the legality of the tracking device placed on the boat in Greece. The Greek officers who assisted with the installation were flown in to testify, along with many other witnesses from around the globe. The Canadian courts are known to be exceptionally lenient when it comes to allowing latitude to the defense and its unconventional arguments against the ironclad evidence presented by prosecutors. Rather than "innocent until proven guilty," law enforcement terms the process "innocent until proven broke." This may sound like jaded police jibe, but one does not have to look any further than extradition requests made by foreign governments such as the 2018 Meng Wanzhou matter that thrust Canada into conflict with China over an American extradition request involving the tech company Huawei. To satisfy an extradition from a country with which Canada has a treaty, the courts are asked to meet the following conditions:

1. Confirm there is reciprocity in charges, meaning the alleged offense against the individual is in fact a criminal offense in Canada.
2. Be satisfied there is sufficient evidence to commit to trial if the offense was to have occurred in Canada.
3. Order the person either released or extradited.

In Canada, extraditions drone on for years—some even lasting over a decade—because the courts allow any and all questioning, even if a rational person would consider the interrogation excessive. In this time of championing human rights, it has never been more evident that the deeper the pockets, the better your chances of skirting justice.

****

It had been my intention to retire in September of 1998, but with the *Blue Dawn* investigation, it was pushed to the end of November. The last three months of my active RCMP service were an intense, seven-day-a-week marathon that could not have been scripted better. I loved the "thrill of the hunt," and this was as good as it got.

In anticipation of retiring from the RCMP, I had obtained a private investigator's license, incorporated, arranged to get office space with a local accounting firm, and put the basic pieces together. I had some trepidation but was committed: there was no turning back at this stage, even though I was forced by circumstances into taking on an even bigger risk by hanging out my own shingle.

When I returned from London, I brought my partner with me to Canada. She, of her own volition, decided to move on to greener pastures with a newfound boyfriend. I had to cash her out of our condominium, which brought with it new debt—an unexpected and added pressure for me, as I had no clients and no revenue stream at the time.

A lesson learned from my failed relationship was in realizing how difficult it is to partner with someone who is coming from a much different culture and socioeconomic background. My partner was from an affluent family in Singapore, and her early life experiences were the polar opposite of mine, which led to a wide gap between our values. The cultural variance can be overcome, but when combined with the value gap, it is an uphill battle. I had seen many red flags along the way but chose to ignore them. I paid the price.

PART TWO
GOING PRIVATE

CHAPTER EIGHT
MAKING THE LEAP & THE EARLY WINS

- Learning the lessons of investing in the present with anticipation of future benefits.
- Taking business risks—much different from the risks taken when with the police.
- Hitting singles rather than home runs.

When incorporating my company in British Columbia, I remember the advice provided by my legal counsel, Tom Russell, who started his own law firm after obtaining his degree. His words of wisdom were, "Hit singles and don't be looking for the home runs." I always kept this sage advice in the back of my mind, and it was consistent with my own thinking. There is no such thing as easy money, and I knew it would take hard work and determination to build a business.

As with any venture, there were some good decisions and some not-so-good ones. Going out on my own was a good one. Way too often, police officers get together with the idea of starting a business together. Perhaps they feel more comfortable with strength of numbers. Often, the business is initially headed up by two or more principals. More often than not, conflicts between the principals emerge, and this is where cracks in the business strategy begin. This can be due to divergent work ethics, different strategies, resistance to investing in the future of the company, or an array of other reasons. Often, the original group gets pared down to one person who embodies the vision for the company.

Trying to do too much is another issue, commonly referred to as "the shotgun approach." Firms offering too many services often find they are not great at any of them, and competitors fill the gaps and become industry leaders. One mistake I made was in choosing an inappropriate company name. West Coast Investigations & Consulting was way too long, sounded parochial, and did not fit with my vision for the company. I disliked the name almost immediately after registering it. In a way, it is like picking a name for a newborn: sometimes you need to get it right, right off the bat.

Rod Stamler encouraged me to set up an offshore entity to help with future covert work he predicted would come my way. This was a big decision at the time, as I had limited capital to work with, and I needed to travel to the Bahamas where an International Business Company (IBC) could be registered, a bank account opened, a credit card obtained, business cards printed, and a mobile phone procured. My story—if anyone asked—was that I was living on my sailboat in Hope Town, Bahamas. An informant from my Miami days was living there, and I simply built off his existence, of course with his approval. It worked: the story appeared real enough while being difficult to crack for anyone looking into my background. The time and money spent to get set up paid dividends for many years. I kept the company going for over ten years and eventually sold it to an undisclosed state spy agency that wanted the legacy I had built.

My original business was run from a small office in an accounting firm. There was not a lot of synergy with the accounting firm, but it was rent-free for the first six months—a good thing, as the early months in business were lean with virtually no revenue.

I initially made the mistake of trying to be all things to all people but realized quickly that it was better to carve out a particular niche and provide specialty services for my clients. In Canada and specifically Vancouver, the private investigation industry is years behind that of New York and London. In the larger centers, there is a mix of professionals in the industry that hail from varied backgrounds, including legal, accounting, secret service, journalism, and, of course, law enforcement. Toronto's private investigation industry is more developed than the rest of Canada's, owing to market size. The bigger players, such as Kroll, Navigant, FTI and others have set up shop in the region to accommodate their clients.

The Vancouver private investigation industry conjures up images of the lone, "gumshoe" detective investigating private matters for private individuals, which is unfortunate. In larger markets, there is more of partnership between investigators and law firms who litigate based on what an investigator turns up. The relationship can work in two ways. Investigators can provide litigation support to a law firm that hires them directly. Second, an investigation firm working for a client can feed a law firm a case where it becomes apparent that evidence will result in litigation. The law firm can then work with the investigation firm's original client. Working in this way allows clients to be shielded by lawyer-client privilege. What passes between an investigator and a lawyer on behalf of a client is protected from disclosure. For this reason, I have often taken cases to law firms. An opportunity developed by me and brought to a law firm can serve the best interest of my client.

ADVANTAGES OF MY FORMER CAREER

I had two distinct advantages: my global network and my undercover skills. One of my first breaks in business was a job at Vancouver International Airport involving one of the companies catering to international airlines. My client company provided required food and duty-free goods replenishment. There were some serious issues to deal with: the theft of duty-free goods, alcohol, and cigarettes, amounting to shrinkage of $25 thousand per week. As well, unionized employees were running roughshod over management. We undertook a two-pronged approach to the problems.

Hidden cameras were secreted in delivery trucks and in the dock areas, and we installed an undercover operator into the mix. I brought in an experienced, retired operator from Scotland Yard by the name of Richard Hester, whom I believed would be the right person for the job. We had to bend a few rules to bring Hester into the country from the UK, and there were the roadblocks thrown up by the union, but we got it done. The hidden camera footage revealed the wholesale theft of goods and the thuggish union culture that existed within the company.

During the evening shifts, some of the employees drank duty-free booze throughout their shifts, and the dock area was deemed a no-go area for management. Management was totally intimidated by the unionized workers, and new hires were quickly browbeaten into submission. Hester was older and not so easily intimidated. He augmented the hidden camera evidence, and forty-five bad actors were identified, of which twenty-five were fired and fifteen disciplined. The ringleader went to jail. It was a great success, and I now had a bank balance with a number with more than one zero after it.

UNDERCOVER AGAIN

I used the undercover technique selectively throughout the years. One of the more enjoyable capers involved a Canadian target who was residing in Costa Rica. The case started in Toronto, where a civil dispute was playing out. In a civil litigation case, there are three distinct stages of the action. First, there is the litigation itself, and if the suit is successful, a judgment is rendered. Second, there is the task of locating assets. Third, there is recovery. Often, this a long, painful process. In this particular case, the defendant was facing a large judgment against him and had used the services of an accountant friend in Costa Rica to hide assets. Funds had been siphoned off from businesses during the litigation process and put in control of the accountant, who acquired bearer certificates. Bearer security occurs when evidence of ownership is provided by possession of the security's certificate. In layperson's terms, this means if you are holding the security, you own it. The issuer keeps no record of ownership. This process requires a leap of faith but works well, as any paper trail comes to a screeching halt once the security is issued.

Through some research, it was determined that the accountant was living in Costa Rica, and a plan to gain access to him was devised. I flew to Miami where a Mountie friend was just finishing up a long-term, joint undercover operation with the FBI. His name was Bill Majcher, and he was game to join me on a trip to Costa Rica. When we met the accountant in northern Costa Rica, ostensibly to discuss property development business, we spun a story about a friend who needed to get funds out of Canada and into an investment that could not be traced. The target took the bait, hook, line, and sinker. He described to us in great detail how he had used an international investment bank and a local bank to move the money, known as layering

(layering hides the source of money with a combination of transactions and bookkeeping maneuvers, where it is finally withdrawn from a legitimate account), and transferred the cash into bearer certificates. The certificates were in turn deposited into a safety deposit box in San Jose. Not only did he tell us how it was done, but we were also introduced to the banker and lawyer who did the dirty work. We handed over the results, gift wrapped, to the plaintiff's lawyer. It was a nice job with some travel and a brilliant conclusion.

SMOKING OUT THE CRIMINALS

A couple of years into my business, I was engaged in what I will label as tobacco work. It was the time frame when "big tobacco" was being attacked from all sides, with a litany of problems to sort out. (I cannot identify the client even though there was extensive public litigation that went on for years.) In all my private investigation experience, the tobacco industry was the most demanding and challenging to please. During a two-year time period, I traveled extensively to the UK, Caribbean, Belize, and throughout North America, where I was tasked to locate people, bank accounts, and assets and identify smuggling schemes. Some of the work was not dissimilar to what I did with the police, with one significant difference: I had no badge or authority. I often sailed close to the wind but knew better than to push the envelope too far. I relied heavily on my global network, always hooking up with a local when arriving in a different country or jurisdiction.

One highlight of the "big tobacco" work involved locating and befriending a tobacco executive who had "gone on the run." First, some context: the *Encyclopedia of Canadian Organized Crime* by Peter Edwards includes the story of Larry Miller (see Further Reading). Miller was an American who had accrued considerable wealth over the years, much of it from tobacco smuggling. Miller would frequent the Sonora Island Lodge, located on British Columbia's West Coast, where cohorts of different stripes would gather to party and scheme. Miller masterminded tobacco smuggling using the Indigenous reserves that straddled the New York and Ontario-Quebec borders. When Canada enacted a two-dollar-a-pack tobacco tax in the early 1990s, it opened up an enormous black market for smuggling cigarettes.

Miller's organization bought untaxed Canadian export cigarettes and hauled them to the border, where they were smuggled back into Canada. It was big business—in the millions. Miller was eventually convicted in the USA and incarcerated for seventeen and a half years. My mission was to locate the former executive who procured the cigarettes that facilitated Miller's smuggling venture. He is referred to as "Fred."

After some time, I managed to locate Fred, who was living in the UK not far from London and still worked in the tobacco industry. In the summer of 2000, I was in the UK working with my ex-Scotland Yard friend, Richard Hester, gathering information and intelligence on Fred, who had acquired considerable wealth during Miller's smuggling days. My big tobacco client was not at all happy with Fred and wanted to learn about his asset accumulation and where to find it. I was able to track down IBCs and bank accounts in Bermuda, but there was more that needed to be done. Through some digging in the UK, we were able to determine Fred had slipped back into Canada where he was visiting his aging father in Vancouver. I quickly made my way back and prepared a plan to befriend Fred.

There is an old saying in undercover work: "When and where." A plan had to be prepared that would allow me an opportunity to engage Fred in a sustainable conversation that could be leveraged into investigative dividends. What better place than on a long-haul flight seated next to Fred? I had learned what day Fred was flying back to London, and it was my intention to get next to him. Originally, he was to be seated in economy, but I knew he would be upgrading. I could not be certain there would be seats in business class available for an upgrade, so I needed a plan. I booked two business class seats and, given that this was pre-9/11, no passport details were required. As anticipated, Fred checked in with the hope of an upgrade at the gate. I was standing in the shadows watching him get the upgrade, and after he left the gate area, I approached the agent and purchased the seat that was next to him. "When and where" was successfully executed. Now I had to get him talking. I had a plan for that as well.

I actually got seated before Fred came onto the plane, and the first thing I did was place a book in the pocket in the back of the seat in front of me with the title exposed, hoping it would catch his eye. The book was titled *Tax Haven Roadmap*. It is a guide for anyone wanting to stash cash offshore. Fred had no sooner seated himself than, even before introducing himself, he asked to look at the book. A nice start to our new relationship.

After Fred perused the book, we began talking. My story was simple but effective. I told Fred I was living on my sailboat in the Caribbean and my specialty was working as a financial adviser. I left things vague enough, allowing Fred to fill in the gaps with his own suppositions. I believe he gathered I was someone of his ilk, with a murky story like many people who hang out in the Caribbean on their sailboats. Almost immediately, Fred began with questions about the best place(s) to register an IBC, the advantages of the different offshore tax havens, and general questions about laundering money and hiding assets. During the flight, Fred was not completely transparent about what he had been up to in the last few years, but enough was said to provide leads for follow-up inquiries. I continued my relationship with Fred for a couple of years. Every encounter provided little gems of information. Eventually I brought my client and Fred together, and they were able to work out an arrangement to mitigate past misdeeds.

ONE BIG CLIENT

While I was involved in the tobacco investigations, I was growing the business, one client at a time. Litigation-supported investigations can be interesting and lucrative, but I was looking for consistent cash flow. Originally this came about through intellectual property investigations. I was able to cultivate Microsoft as a client, and I became their go-to guy on the West Coast. Microsoft, like all software producers, had problems with counterfeiters who would knock off their product. I was engaged to do a number of things, including mystery shopping, conducting sweeps, and following up on tips that came in anonymously. We also set up a physical storefront software business that was used when doing undercover investigations and provided an air of legitimacy for our inquiries.

During those years I had computer technicians who did my information technology (IT) work when required. One such technician, Amir, was a curious individual with an interest in the covert work I was doing. What better person to groom as an undercover operative for the storefront? He was originally from Iran and had fled the country under the cover of darkness with the assistance of people smugglers. Being caught would have meant almost certain execution on the spot. After leaving Iran, he stayed in a safe house in Pakistan for two weeks, eventually making his way to Sweden on a bogus Spanish passport. In Sweden, he learned that he could obtain residency in Canada by flashing his Iranian passport on arrival and making a refugee claim. And that is exactly what he did after touching down in Calgary. Amir turned out to be a wonderful addition to Canada and, luckily for me, he was good at IT and undercover work. He became a good friend.

After a couple of years, I moved my business to central Vancouver and started to share space with Pat McParland and Jim Blatchford, both forensic accountants who had previously been working with large, global accounting firms. Sharing space with McParland and Blatchford made good economic sense, plus our skill sets overlapped on some of the work that came in.

TO SELL OR NOT TO SELL?

In 2002, IPSA International came calling. IPSA was an offshoot of a security guard company that had been built from the ground up in the San Francisco Bay Area by Tom Keating. After selling the security business for $300 million, he sank some of the profits into IPSA, a corporate investigations company. Keating brought his son in as the CEO and his daughter as the CFO. When IPSA acquired my company, there were established offices in Toronto, Chicago, New York, Miami, Atlanta, Boston, Dallas, Los Angeles, Seattle, San Francisco, and Phoenix, where the HQ was located. The decision to sell was a difficult one for me. Relinquishing control of my company meant others would be making the ultimate decisions going forward and had the potential to have negative impact on what I was building in Vancouver. I would become a smaller fish in a bigger pond.

Nevertheless, I needed a cash infusion, having taken on new debt when I first started the company, and I saw it as a way to scale up. Growing a company organically is challenging, and it can take many years to establish yourself, especially in a small marketplace like Vancouver. I decided to sell and was able to negotiate one important provision. IPSA was offering an "earn out": one-third of the sale price would be paid out initially, and then the other two-thirds had to be earned out. I was given three years to accomplish the earn out. The compromise was IPSA would let me have a certain amount of autonomy during the earn-out period, maximizing my chances of getting all of the money out of the deal. It was a win-win situation. I had low overhead and a decent stable of clients, and ran an efficient ship that yielded constant profits.

During my early years with IPSA, many of its offices were not doing so well. By the time the third year rolled around, we were down to half the offices and a much leaner team. It was a win for the buyers because they actually acquired my company by only having to spend the original one-third down payment. The other two-thirds came from the profits I made over the first couple of years.

One big thing that was a draw for me to sell was the opportunity to expand my horizons. Scaling up in the Vancouver market would be difficult unless I was prepared to bring outside money into the mix. Building a successful company was going to be a long journey. I was no longer a young man.

CHAPTER NINE
THE IPSA ROLLER COASTER RIDE

- Business development: not an easy thing to accomplish.
- Saved by a Russian entrepreneur.
- Back to my old stomping grounds in London.

Earlier, I made reference to the usefulness of undercover skills honed while in the service of the RCMP for developing business in the private sector. I would rate my undercover skills as average to a bit above average. I had some reasonable successes, but I did not consider myself in the top echelon. I would say most of us in the RCMP were journeymen with the occasional star investigator rising to the top. It was not that much different from playing with a hockey team: many players are the supporting cast for a couple of ringers. My business development style mirrored how I conducted undercover work. I was a plodder and called what I did "stalking." That sounds sinister, but it wasn't. It was simply a method of targeting new business. With a business plan laid out in my mind, I would carefully "stalk" opportunities as they presented themselves.

To have a successful business, one needs a steady cash flow. It is very difficult to execute a strategic plan if you can't accurately predict the revenues. My plan was to build on developing revenues from due diligence investigations. Vancouver is not a financial center where there are many banks in need of due diligence service providers, and this made things more challenging. Only the Hong Kong Savings Bank of Canada (HSBC) had its headquarters in Vancouver. The rest of the global banks were based in Toronto, and, to a lesser extent, in Montreal. To raise my profile in this area, I became an active board member of the Vancouver chapters of the Association of Certified Fraud Examiners (ACFE) and the Association of Certified Anti-Money Laundering Specialists (ACAMS). The local chapters would host monthly luncheons, and I volunteered to find guest speakers.

Finding good speakers was not an easy task, but it did fit into my business development plan. Identifying and recruiting people in the business community to present at events served the chapter well and also afforded me the opportunity to cold call and engage people in conversations. This would often lead to a lunch date. Most people have a low tolerance for a sales pitch, and that was something I avoided. My *modus operandi* was to simply engage in conversation and develop a rapport that would sometimes lead to a business opportunity. I was building the business by hitting singles, not swinging for the fence.

SAVING THE COMPANY

By the third year with IPSA, it became evident many of the offices were not going to be around much longer. In 2005 the Keating family decided it was not going to continue bleeding money, and the company was sold for a modest amount of money to Dan Wachtler, a vice-president at IPSA. Many of the branch offices were chopped, including some that survived the first cut but not a second one.

Then along came 2008 and the global financial meltdown. In 2008, the Vancouver office had its first unprofitable quarter, even though I had the most successful office in the company. Wachtler had mortgaged everything to keep things going, including his home, and we had just enough funds to make one or maybe two pay cycles. With "two out, two strikes, in the bottom of the ninth," I hit one out of the park.

In February 2010, on a Sunday evening, I received a call from my old friend Bill Majcher, the same investigator who traveled with me to Costa Rica on another case (see Chapter Eight). He had left the RCMP and was living in Hong Kong, where he worked with a financial firm that put deals together and took companies public. Majcher had an entrepreneurial side that made him a good undercover operator, and his business acumen was something most law enforcement people lack. He also had an extensive Rolodex.

When Majcher called, he was in London with an unnamed Dutchman and a Russian national, Vladimir Antonov. The two Europeans were in the process of purchasing Saab from General Motors, and during the negotiations some negative media came out about Antonov. An article had appeared in a second-tier Swedish newspaper by a journalist who normally did not write about business topics. The article claimed that Antonov was heavily involved in Russian organized crime, and General Motors put a halt on the deal because of the allegations made in the paper. Majcher asked me when I could come to London, and I replied that if Antonov was serious, he could purchase a business class ticket for me, and I would fly out the next day. The ticket arrived in the morning, and I was on a night flight Monday evening heading for Heathrow.

Prior to departing for London, I conducted a cursory search on Antonov through a subcontractor who did work for IPSA in the Former Soviet Union (FSU). Before I was going to engage with a Russian national, I did my own due diligence. There were no apparent reputational issues with him or his businesses.

Flights going from Vancouver to Heathrow leave later in the day, and there are approximately ten hours in the air and an eight-hour time difference. I arrived midday on Tuesday and was in the City (the financial district) on Lombard Street meeting with several people a couple of hours later. Antonov was in his mid-thirties and operated from a recently established bank he owned. He was reported to be worth $300 million, but I later learned his net worth was closer to $3 billion. Antonov was too young to be around when the oligarchs were vacuuming up Russian state assets for themselves. The Antonov Group comprised turnaround specialists and started making money around 2000. Much of it came from the banking sector.

General Motors had halted all negotiations with Antonov, even though he refuted the public accusations and asked to have an opportunity to clear his name. That is where IPSA came into the picture. In the industry, hiring a firm to conduct due diligence on your own business and people is called a "commissioned report." With Antonov as my client, I would be engaged to conduct an independent investigation into all of his holdings and people.

This was no simple task; he owned assets in numerous countries, and there were over forty people who were managers and shareholders that we were to conduct due diligence on.

After spending most of the week in London, I came away with a shopping list of things requiring my immediate attention, many of which later came out in the Swedish media. They included:

- conducting an investigation in Sweden to determine who was behind the organized crime stories being spread about Antonov;
- conducting inquiries with law enforcement in the UK, USA, and Russia to determine whether there were any indicators of an organized crime association;
- conducting inquiries with regulators in the Baltic countries where Antonov owned banks to determine whether there were any money laundering issues;
- conducting inquiries in Russia to learn more about an assassination attempt that was made on Antonov's father;
- determining how the Antonovs were able to accumulate their wealth in a short, ten-year period of time;
- traveling to Panama and Dominica, where banks had recently been acquired, and meeting with regulators to determine whether there were any money laundering issues;
- traveling to St. Kitts & Nevis to substantiate an asset owned by the Antonov Group;
- meeting with Swiss and British banks in London to determine whether there were any issues concerning the image of the Antonov Group; and
- conducting due diligence on all managers and shareholders of the Antonov Group.

Prior to returning to Vancouver, I presented Antonov with a $150-thousand retainer invoice and made it known that I would commence with the work as soon as the money hit my account. It was there within a couple of days. This was the lifeline IPSA needed to keep its head above water. Over the next three months, I was pretty much in travel mode. I brought along a colleague to assist me, and, in total, we traveled to nine different countries including the UK, USA, Latvia, Lithuania, Sweden, Russia, Panama, Dominica, and St. Kitts and Nevis.

There were thirteen reputational issues that came out in the media, albeit that most of them were in Russian publications. It is commonplace in Russia to have your business enemies orchestrate negative media reports by paying off journalists in an effort to tarnish images and influence public opinion. We were also able to determine the reason behind an attempted assassination of Antonov's father, which was due to a dispute over a banking asset that a crime group was attempting to take control of. The people behind the attempt were in fact Chechens, organized criminals of the worst kind; they were attempting to extort $100 million from the Antonov Group. It was after the assassination attempt that Antonov moved to London and his father moved to Lithuania from Moscow. Antonov Senior had been shot several times, and luckily, he survived, but his driver did not.

CLEARING OUR CLIENT'S NAME

One of Antonov's priorities was to find out who was behind the media stories that surfaced in Sweden. The journalist writing most of the stories was someone who normally specialized in home and garden articles, and writing about a major business deal was out of the ordinary for them. In reading the articles, it became apparent that the Swedish journalist did little actual research other than rehashing Russian articles that had been written about the Antonov Group, including the assassination attempt. The attempt was a typical extortion plot that was reported to the authorities, who did as little as possible to assist in finding the perpetrators. Another debunked story involved a Moldovan wine merchant who died owing money to an Antonov-owned bank. The piece appeared in the Russian media alleging that Antonov orchestrated the killing. The truth was much different: the wine merchant ran into major financial difficulties when Russia imposed tariffs on wine imports from Moldova. The investigating officer told us he had died by suicide.

Getting to the bottom of matters in Russia can be very challenging and hazardous, and one must tread lightly to avoid attracting the attention of the wrong people. In Russia, corruption permeates society, including law enforcement. The Foreign Security Service (FSB) is tasked with investigating organized crime and dealing with national security issues. The FSB is notoriously corrupt and viewed as the strong arm for Vladimir Putin's government.

After determining the Swedish journalist did nothing more than cobble stories together from other sources while adding a negative spin, the next step was to determine what the motive was. To accomplish our objectives, we decided to conduct an undercover investigation of the journalist. Ultimately, the naive journalist disclosed that a high-ranking Swedish bureaucrat was behind the stories, motivated only by not wanting the iconic Swedish car brand to end up being partially owned by a young Russian entrepreneur. Unfortunately, I am not able to disclose how we were able to accomplish our objectives, but I can say it went a long way in clearing Antonov's name and his being able to reinsert himself into the deal with GM.

In Dominica and Panama, we were able to determine that the banks acquired by Antonov had been experiencing financial difficulties prior to being acquired. The acquisitions were consistent with the business model used successfully in other countries; he recognized an opportunity to turn around a failing business by inserting new technology and effective management while supporting the banks through the network of his other businesses. In both locations, the regulators were happy to see the new ownership making meaningful improvements.

Traveling to Moscow and Vilnius, Lithuania was a bit nostalgic for me. My last trip to these countries had been in 1997, and things had changed considerably in both locations, but in different ways. In Moscow in the 1990s, most Russians were driving Ladas, and many were using public transportation to get around. When I returned in 2010, there were few Ladas on the roads, and most vehicles were imports of some sort. Over the thirteen years since my last trip to Moscow, many Russians had acquired vehicles, and the road traffic was horrendous. Our flight arrived at Sheremetyevo International Airport at around noon, and it took us three hours to drive to the city center.

Normally this was a thirty-minute drive. It was gridlocked most of the way. On March 29, a couple of weeks before arriving in Moscow, there had been a horrific suicide bombing at two subway stations that killed forty people and injured another hundred. I surmised this was the reason for the gridlock, thinking no one was using the airport train. However, I was told the traffic was normally jammed during the middle of the day due to the ubiquity of cars and the lack of investment in road infrastructure.

In Vilnius, the experience was a pleasant surprise. My first trip there was in November 1993, when things were grim. Lithuania and the other two Baltic countries had recently obtained independence, and the moribund economies were in transition mode from communism to capitalism. The week I arrived in 1993, a journalist had been assassinated by organized crime as retribution for negative stories that he had written. There had just been a wholesale changeover in law enforcement personnel; the old Russian guard had been kicked out and were replaced by young, inexperienced Lithuanians. It was close to anarchy.

I was staying in a dilapidated Soviet-era-style hotel where the clerk spoke no English, the elevators did not work, and brown water came out of the taps. To compound the situation, just after dark, power in the entire city was shut down due to production shortages. I remember walking three blocks to one of the few restaurants that were open, being guided by a single light bulb run off a local generator. It was an eerie feeling. When I returned in 2010, I stayed in a beautiful boutique hotel in the old town that had been refurbished, and the scene was energetic. It was a good feeling to see how foreign direct investment had turned a dour situation into a vibrant, upbeat city.

The inquiries and research were documented in a two-hundred-page report that was submitted to General Motors and the financial institutions that were providing funding to the deal. The entire project generated $500 thousand in revenues and went a long way in allowing IPSA to stay in existence. Antonov posted the report on the company website for all to see, and eventually, the Saab deal was closed. Preparing a commissioned report can be challenging, especially if negative reputational information surfaces during the inquiries. I told Antonov before engaging with the project that ethically we were compelled to report our findings in a transparent manner. Fortunately, this did not become an issue.

Vladimir Antonov was a modern, highly intelligent Russian who, as you would expect, was a big risk-taker. You don't go from zero to being a billionaire in a few short years without being a risk-taker. Although his success spoke for itself, Antonov did acknowledge that he had to change how he conducted business, and given that he was now a London businessman, he wanted to engage a risk manager. He offered the job to me after we submitted our report. I considered taking the position, but his reckless business style caused me some concern, and I did not accept the offer—a fortunate decision.

The following was reported by the *Business Insider* on December 12, 2011:

> *Antonov, along with his Lithuanian partner Raimondas Baranauskas, was arrested in London on November 23, and charged in connexion with a Lithuanian extradition warrant. In Lithuania, they are accused of embezzlement of several hundred million dollars from Bank Snoras, the bank they control in Lithuania, and the second largest in that country. The forensic auditors are reported to have found that Snoras's books were short by 1.4 billion dollars.*

I learned that the missing money was eventually accounted for, but this did not stop the extradition process, and eventually, Antonov was ordered by the courts to be extradited to Lithuania. Antonov was out on bail at the time of the court decision, and he went "on the run" and is reportedly living in Russia. His reckless behavior got the better of him.

The last time I met with Antonov was in London in early 2012. He still had his sense of humor, relating the following to me: on the day of his arrest, he had just flown into the UK and was clearing customs when he learned about his problem in Lithuania. He said, "I went from my private plane to my private cell." That made us both chuckle.

FLIGHT TAKES OFF WITH NO CONFIRMED SEAT FOR IPSA

Financial turbulence was not the only bumpy ride for IPSA. On May 29, 2006 reports in the media indicated Air Canada (AC) and WestJet (WJ) had settled legal disputes that had been festering for a couple of years. The media reports represented a conclusion to a high-profile industrial espionage story that started in 2004 when AC corporate security contacted IPSA International with a request to assist with an ongoing problem they had with their competitor, WJ. It was reported that WJ apologized to AC and paid $15.5 million to settle a lawsuit over a case of corporate espionage. The behind-the-scenes story leading to the two airlines' public resolution was one that most people are not aware of. Several media stories were published on the espionage saga, including one by *Maclean's* magazine on September 20, 2004.

In 2004, I was contacted by Yves Duguay, who was in charge of corporate security for Air Canada. I first met Duguay in the 1980s when I was running the RCMP Undercover Program and when he successfully completed the course as an operator. My involvement with him, when we worked a case involving a cooperating source I developed in Miami who was sent to Bolivia to arrange a cocaine shipment to Canada, is detailed in Chapter Four. Duguay and I had an amicable relationship and one of mutual respect. His current problem was complicated and required the services of an investigation firm that he could trust.

AC had learned that WJ was accessing AC's private files online and using the information to WJ's business advantage. AC believed its flight-load data was being compromised (this is industry jargon for the number of passengers flying on specific flights). The information accessed gave insight into which routes made money and which did not—invaluable information in a business built on tight margins. The information went a long way to answering questions about why WJ was making all the recent right strategic decisions, such as flipping its Montreal-Vancouver flight from evening to morning.

The IPSA investigation focused on Mark Hill, a co-founder of WJ who lived in Oak Bay, an upmarket residential area in the greater Victoria area on Vancouver Island. IPSA was asked to conduct background inquiries into Hill to learn more about his daily business activities. Surveillance was conducted on his residence, and it provided little helpful information other than the observation that Hill put his garbage out weekly, and that it was picked up by the garbage disposal company used by the municipality. Hill lived on a cul-de-sac shared with approximately ten other detached homes. Under Canadian law, when a person sets their trash out on the street for pickup, the courts consider that one's expectation to privacy with respect to the garbage is relinquished. In other words, discarded trash is fair game.

Picking up a target's trash is colloquially referred to as "dumpster diving" and has been going on for decades. It has paid dividends on many investigations, but in recent years there have been people doing it with more sinister motives to obtain unsuspecting personal information in order to create false identities. Our motive was to determine whether Hill was throwing out any AC documents that he was wrongfully gaining access to through covert activities.

The cul-de-sac where Hill lived was not an easy place to do pickups, and on the second retrieval Hill emerged from his house and snapped a picture of the IPSA investigators. While taking the pictures, he yelled out, "Are you working for Air Canada?" These pictures were subsequently printed in newspapers, and the incident initially gave Hill and WJ something to be indignant about. Apparently, Hill's neighbor had observed our people, and this caused suspicion. Between the two pickups we completed, there was nothing of interest other than enough shredded documents to fill a large garbage bag. The shredding was done with a cross-cut machine, which meant the pieces were small. Through a contact of mine we established that there was a firm in Houston called Church Technologies that had the ability to digitally reconstitute the shredded documents. It was not cheap: we paid $20 thousand for the work required on the contents of the bag. It turned out to be money well spent, as the contents of the bag contained confidential AC load documents.

Prior to getting caught out doing the trash pickup, we also had an opportunity to put an investigator in a seat beside Hill, who was flying on AC 908 from Toronto to Florida. The IPSA investigator, Bob Stenhouse, who was another undercover course attendee in 1987, was the person we tasked with the engagement. Even though Hill, whose title was Vice President of Strategic Planning at WJ, was in enemy territory on an AC flight, he was unconcerned about reviewing AC load documents on his laptop next to Stenhouse.

As if tempting fate, Hill also wore a WJ denim shirt and a leather jacket with a large WJ logo on the back. This was a good entry point for Bob to start a conversation with Hill but turned out not to be overly productive other than determining Hill's overt disdain for AC. However, Stenhouse did observe Hill opening a manila envelope from which he pulled out sheets of paper and entered data into his laptop. The data for February 2004 included flight numbers, departure and arrival times, and load capacities. It was later determined the numbers 100, 101, 104, and 125 matched AC and Jetsgo flights. Stenhouse observed Hill entering this and more information into a program on his laptop.

The investigation moved quickly at the end, and AC's legal team was anxious to obtain affidavits from our investigators who had critical information in support of the anticipated legal action against WJ.

CYA—ALWAYS

Early on in the investigation I had presented a Letter of Engagement (LOE) to Duguay that contained standard language about indemnification. Case law in Canada states that if an agent (such as IPSA), when following instructions from a client (such as AC), is exposed to legal action, the client is required to indemnify the agent. In other words, the client pays for the agent's legal defense should any lawsuit brought against an agent arise, along with any settlement, if successful, on the plaintiff's part. When I brought it to Duguay's attention that our LOE had yet to be signed, he assured me indemnification would not be an issue and once the agreement was reviewed by AC's general counsel it would be duly signed and returned. Given this assurance, I gave our investigators the green light to swear the affidavits. As it turned out, I was too trusting.

AC sued WJ, which in turn countersued both AC and IPSA. WJ's contention was that Hill's privacy had been breached because Hill's residence was on a private cul-de-sac that was common property belonging collectively to the homeowners, and therefore not part of the municipality of Oak Bay. There were no signs indicating the cul-de-sac was private property: it had a street name and the appearance of being a regular public street. However, picking up Hill's trash on a private cul-de-sac could technically be construed as an infringement of his privacy. Second, Hill had shredded the documents to ensure they were not to be read by any third parties. By reconstructing the documents, we had notionally violated his privacy.

The first contention was an oversight by IPSA that we felt could be successfully defended, and the second contention of reassembling shredded documents had never been argued before in the Canadian courts; thus it was hard to predict what the outcome would be.

IPSA had followed the instructions provided by AC, resulting in obtaining critical evidence allowing AC to follow through with legal action putting a stop to WJ's activities. I am not sure if Duguay knew of AC's intentions when he assured me IPSA would be indemnified, but in the end AC's strategy became clear. They cut us adrift and would condemn our actions if need be. We could have in turn sued AC for non-indemnification, which would have meant that IPSA then would have had to finance two costly lawsuits. Not a nice move on AC's part, but in the big scheme of things, the company was not overly concerned about IPSA.

If you get caught up in the Canadian court system, you can be assured of two things. Your bank account will take a significant hit, and there will be considerable frustration. I am saying this from my first-hand experiences, and also from listening to friends, clients, and others who had the unfortunate experience of being party to cases being heard in civil, criminal, probate, and family courts. The effectiveness of our courts has been on a slippery slope since the *Constitution Act, 1982* (part of Canada's constitution) was enacted. Litigators I have worked with over the years have told me going to court is a crapshoot. I feel our courts are not part of a "justice" system. Instead, I consider our courts part of a "legal" system, and an unpredictable one at that. Too many judges are appointed for politically correct reasons. There are several examples of appointments to the Supreme Court of Canada where the appointee had never sat as a judge at any level. Perplexing.

In Jonathan Manthorpe's book, *Restoring Democracy in an Age of Populists and Pestilence* (see Further Reading), he opines on what has occurred post-1982 constitution:

> *There is no question that on occasion, armed with the Charter of Rights and Freedoms, the Supreme Court and other senior provincial courts have exceeded their proper role in Canadian public life. It is important to recognize, however, that that is because of a failure of Canadian political life, not a coup by the judges. By assuming the role of defenders of individual rights and aspirations, they filled a vacuum created by a deficient political system.*

IPSA was spared the wrath of the legal system and being a pawn stuck between two corporate heavyweights that had the resources to hire serious litigators. It could have been ugly.

A NEW REVENUE STREAM

My original business plan was to build a steady stream of due diligence revenues—the Antonov project was an anomaly. Another one of my first breakthroughs in this respect happened when I was engaged by HSBC in Vancouver, providing due diligence reports on applicants who were seeking to gain entry to Canada by way of the Federal Immigrant Investor Program. Eric Major, who was the global head of HSBC's immigrant investor section, was looking to improve the compliance standards for his bank and also for industry as a whole.

Canada and Quebec had long-established programs that attracted applicants who, for different reasons, wanted to establish themselves and their families in a country with a bright future. There are many wealthy countries offering similar programs that provide the right to residency leading to citizenship. The entire process can take three to five years, and the programs are called Residency by Investment (RBI). There are other smaller countries—five of which are in the Caribbean—that offer citizenship within three to six months. These programs are referred to as a Citizenship by Investment (CBI). There are many different programs offered by numerous countries, and they are all lumped into what is called the Immigrant Investor Industry (III). Major was a significant player in the industry and opened up new opportunities for a new revenue stream.

CHAPTER TEN
THE LONDON-CARIBBEAN EXPERIENCE

- IPSA's transition from the brink to a bonanza.
- The Libyan caper, a case study in extreme risk management.
- IPSA generates huge revenues through "look-back" projects and the Immigrant Investor Industry.

The IPSA that acquired me and my company in 2002 had a much different look by the time 2011 rolled around. When I started, there were several offices spread around North America, including the Vancouver and Toronto offices. Now we had the Vancouver office, Phoenix as the administrative center, and New York. The New York office had a few full-time people, and the business model was driven by big "look-back" projects. A "look back" is essentially an anti-money-laundering audit of the transactions completed over a period of time, normally a few years. When the financial meltdown happened in 2008, American regulators eased up on financial institutions (FIs) to help them recover from financial shock. The compliance honeymoon came to an end in 2010. Regulators started sanctioning banks again with huge fines as well as compelling them to conduct "look backs." Global FIs conduct thousands of transactions every week, and the resources required for complete reviews are considerable.

Dan Wachtler, CEO of IPSA, was good at business development, and his efforts resulted in creating large, revenue-generating opportunities that normally took several months to complete. IPSA USA had an extensive Rolodex of people who were contracted to go on-site and complete the compliance work required post-2010. An engagement sometimes required as many as one hundred or more people. The margins on the work were thin, but with the volume of work there was considerable profit.

In the meantime, Vancouver had improved its bottom line handsomely, with monthly gross revenues in the $100-thousand range. The office was now conducting considerably more global due diligence work, requiring a few new hires with research capabilities.

In early 2011, IPSA intended to extend its global reach, and London was chosen as the first location for expansion. IPSA, like most global due diligence service providers, used a network of subcontractors to assist with completing inquiries. IPSA had a trusted subcontractor in London, and consideration was being given to acquire this firm to get a foothold in the UK market. Dan and I traveled to London in early 2011 in pursuit of the acquisition, which, unfortunately, did not come to fruition. That was when Wachtler asked if I would consider moving there to establish an office.

Moving to London was an attractive opportunity, but I had some concerns around what this meant for me personally as I was now closing in on sixty years of age. I was also married with two stepdaughters, the younger having just finished high school. The older daughter was attending the University of Victoria. Everyone in the family was keen to participate in a new life adventure, but it was the challenge of opening a new office and generating revenues that concerned me. London, as a global financial center, has many due diligence service providers, competition was going to be stiff, plus I was not a local. I was also tasked with opening offices in Dubai and Hong Kong. If that was not enough, I would be expected to return to Vancouver on a monthly basis to ensure things were not going off the rails. We had some good talent in the office, but no one was ready to take over as managing director. There would be a lot of jet time.

EAT WHAT YOU KILL

One critical aspect of building a business and establishing it is hiring the right person at the managing director level. This sounds like it should be simple, but it is not. My success rate over the years doing this is around 50 percent.

IPSA had evolved into being primarily a risk management company with the services tailored for the financial industry. To find a person who can step into a role of developing business is no easy task. The good ones normally either work for a competitor earning large fees or have broken away to focus attention on building their own businesses. To entice a person to make the leap requires a good plan and a fat wallet. I knew several people who were making the transition from law enforcement to the private sector; they were good people but had no proven record with business development, and very often this was their Achilles' heel. Then there are the ones who have worked for large, global firms who want to get away from the politics and bureaucracy. Many of these people cannot make the transition to being a managing director at a smaller firm, as they are used to being fed opportunities instead of developing business for themselves. With small firms, you "eat what you kill." In London, we ultimately hired Hugo Williamson, who had been with a larger firm and had broken away to start a business with his father, a retired MI6 officer. IPSA piqued Williamson's interest, and he onboarded with us. In Hong Kong, we hired Trevor Collins, a retired Royal Hong Kong Police (RHKP) officer with loads of experience in the private sector. Both turned out to be good managing directors.

THE PAST CATCHES UP

In March 2013, Wachtler and I were in Dubai setting up an entity and scouring the terrain for a managing director who could get things moving in the right direction. That is when I received an unexpected communication from "Perry," the Canadian who got locked up when I was running things in Miami for the RCMP, and who eventually became a cooperating informant (see Chapter Four). Perry had located me through a Google search and had some information about stolen Libyan booty that he thought might interest me. It had been twenty years or more since I had had any contact with him.

Perry provided some details about the opportunity. His buddy, another Canadian of the same ilk as Perry, was residing in Bangkok, where he came into contact with an African who was working at an embassy in Bangkok. The African diplomat, in turn, had a cousin who was a former brigadier general in the Sudanese army. He knew people who were holding $240 million that had been removed from Libya when things unraveled politically in the country. This investigation was written up in the anti-money-laundering trade magazine for professionals in the field, *ACAMS Today*, in an article titled "Lured by $240 million of stolen Libyan cash." The African diplomat was not aware of who I actually was, and my intent was to repatriate the money to Libya if we confirmed that that was where it was stolen from.

In February 2011, the Libyan Arab Spring kicked off in an effort to oust Colonel Muammar Gaddafi, who was determined to hang onto power. During the confusion of the insurgency, Gaddafi's wife and three children escaped to Algeria and, reportedly, $160 billion in state assets was smuggled out of the country. The search was on for the $160 billion, and international organizations joined to locate and repatriate the missing assets. This included the World Bank, having initiated the creation of a unit itself called STAR (for "stolen asset recovery"), tasked with assisting countries that were endeavoring to recover state assets. The new Libyan government had also contracted private financial investigators to locate assets and manage the legal hurdles to repatriate them.

Our end goal was to negotiate a contract with the Libyan government, but there were many hurdles to clear before we could do this. An article titled "Recovering Stolen Assets: Making a Hash of Finding the Cash" featured in *The Economist* in May 2013 about addressed this topic. I heard more than one story about supposed caches of money around Africa; the trick was to establish if there was validity to the stories.

After being introduced on the phone to the Canadian in Bangkok, we learned the money had been removed from Libya via tanker truck and driven to Abidjan, Ivory Coast, where it was being stored in a warehouse near the international airport. The controllers of the money were prepared to relinquish 40 percent of the funds to a partner who could physically remove the cash, launder it, and deposit the remaining 60 percent into offshore accounts. This was going to be a monumental task. Before any final decisions on our involvement could be made, many matters needed to be determined, including:

- the accuracy of the information (Was it legitimate or a scam? Was the money counterfeit?);

- how to negotiate with the asset controllers who were located in a corrupt country with no rule of law;
- how to conduct a stolen property investigation without the luxury of being law enforcement;
- how to fund the investigation, as we did not have a client to underwrite an investigation of this magnitude; and
- how to generate cooperating interest with international organizations and law enforcement.

Wachtler was certainly not averse to risk, and we had good rapport along with a mutual trust level. He agreed to have IPSA fund the investigation until a contract could be sourced. We needed a partner to work with, and Martin Kenney came immediately to mind. Martin's brother, Jason Kenney, was a well-known politician in Canada. Martin had a long history of working cases with IPSA and had a reputation as an internationally acclaimed asset recovery specialist. He lived and worked from the British Virgin Islands, where we met to discuss the opportunity.

Another bonus with having Kenney on board was that he had recently been working with the World Bank on similar projects involving Middle Eastern countries. We agreed to co-finance the investigation until we could determine if the funds, in fact, belonged to the Libyan state, and then we would approach the officials there about repatriating the money for them. Kenney's team would work on the legalities, and IPSA would conduct the investigation. If we did manage to repatriate the $240 million, our take would be $96 million that would be split among our two firms and the people who brought the opportunity to me. The Canadian in Bangkok, his Australian mate who had co-developed the opportunity, and the African diplomat would need to be cut in on the deal.

After several phone calls and our conducting our research, I boarded a plane from London to Bangkok, where I met the duo. Things progressed quickly after my arrival. I was covertly introduced to the diplomat, who put me on a secure phone call to the Sudanese brigadier general. I pitched myself to the diplomat as a trusted friend of the Bangkok-based Canadian and said that I lived in the UK and worked in the financial industry. I claimed that I possessed the contacts, experience, and ability to transport and launder the money. The diplomat seemed comfortable with my pitch.

As the investigation moved along, the story was that we would fly into Ivory Coast from Malta, pick up the funds, and fly back to Malta, where they would be stored and bled into Monaco casinos through our contacts. Of course, this was easier said than done, but we had to demonstrate there was a plan.

The asset controllers eagerly invited us to Abidjan, where we would be able to see the money and satisfy ourselves that it physically existed. We decided to send the diplomat, and his instructions from me were very clear: verify, verify, verify. This meant asking questions, observing, getting samples, taking pictures, and gleaning all possible intelligence that would allow for authentication. Upon arrival in Abidjan, the diplomat was taken to a bonded warehouse near the main airport, Port Bouët, and was shown a large container stacked full of $100 bills, totaling $20 million.

He was allowed to randomly take samples and pictures to satisfy himself that the box was full of genuine currency. The box showed Arabic writing on sealing tape and had a label bearing the coat of arms of Gaddafi's Great Socialist People's Libyan Arab Jamahiriya (roughly translated to "state of the masses"). The diplomat was told there were eleven more boxes, each containing the same number of bills, and, as long as one of their people accompanied the funds, they could be loaded up and flown out of the country. This was an encouraging first step.

Contact was made with the U.S. Secret Service that has the global mandate to investigate matters involving American currency. After considerable deliberation it was concluded that the money was legitimate and other information about the provenance of the bills was disclosed. The Secret Service informed us that the U.S. Federal Reserve Banks send bulk cash in $100 denominations boxed exactly like the ones shown in our photographs, except, of course, for the Arabic tape and Libyan crest. Bulk American currency like this is routinely shipped to large banks in Zurich and London, where it is then supplied to central banks located in Africa and elsewhere. The Secret Service was also able to analyze the serial numbers on the notes and determined they had been shipped from New York to Zurich in 2013. This was the first red flag, considering Gaddafi had been executed in October 2011.

Cunning Edge

A picture taken of "stolen" Libyan state assets in the form of American currency. At the beginning of our investigation, we took samples and pictures. A box shows Arabic writing on sealing tape and a label bearing the coat of arms of Gaddafi's Great Socialist People's Libyan Arab Jamahiriya.

I returned to Bangkok on a second trip to meet the Canadian and his Australian sidekick, as well as the diplomat. At the second meeting with the diplomat, I drilled down on what had transpired in Abidjan and whom he had met. It was evident that the Ivory Coast people whom the diplomat had met were in control of the assets and were calling the shots. They had colluded with other military colleagues in the region to advance the situation to its current status. Apparently, there was $240 million currently in storage in Abidjan, and considerably more money was being held in Burkina Faso, north of Ivory Coast, and was going to be eventually transported to the coast. When I questioned the diplomat about the viewing of the box of money and who was present in the warehouse, he told me there were uniformed guards in the room. This seemed unusual, as one would expect less official-looking guardianship from a group of money launderers.

There was a lot of background work that needed to be done to advance the project, including coordinating with the World Bank in an effort to get the preliminary work done for when, and if, we determined the money belonged to Libya. Coordination with the U.S. Secret Service was imperative; we would potentially be taking control of huge amounts of American currency, and the Secret Service had to be in the loop. Plus, when possible, we would be provided with intelligence on how bulk cash was moved globally.

There was also the transportation component. Flying the money out of Ivory Coast would be challenging. I spoke to former British military service people who did government mercenary work. I was assured it could be done in the middle of the night with ground support by the French Foreign Legion; it was not going to be cheap. Flight plans needed careful coordination between Malta and Abidjan, where the cash would be loaded sometime after midnight and before the airport reopened at o'clock in the morning. The aircraft would need to refuel in Abidjan and return to Malta. There was also coordination to be done on arrival in Malta, and the in-country authorities needed to be briefed on our plan, along with arrangements made to secure the money on arrival. Tripoli, Libya was just 350 kilometers (218 miles) from Malta, and it would be a convenient location to hand over the assets when we got to that stage.

The investigative team concluded that travel to Abidjan a second time was necessary to glean more information, gather logistical details, identify more of the players, and further validate the existence of the asset. That was when I decided to bring my former colleague, Bill Majcher, into the fray. Fortuitously, Majcher had been dealing with an Ivory Coast national on a deal, and this person had previously invited him to travel there to further the discussions. This was the perfect scenario, as Majcher would need a visa, which would be facilitated by his business associate. While there, Majcher would be my second set of eyes and ears. The diplomat and the Australian would also be traveling to Abidjan. The diplomat was a known person, and the Australian, who had previously worked in an air cargo business, would be able to determine the weight and size of the boxes for the extraction and be able to assist with verification. Majcher would lay low until the viewing was completed and then meet with the currency controllers to negotiate terms. It seemed like we had a secure plan, at least for the next stage.

The subsequent trip occurred in October 2013, and after waiting around for three days, the Aussie and diplomat were taken to the same warehouse and shown four boxes of money, again accompanied by the uniformed guards. We had been promised to be shown twelve boxes.

The Aussie meticulously took pictures, obtained samples, took measurements, and gathered information. After the viewing, Majcher met with the controllers to discuss how the handover would work. Eventually he flew up to London, where he was debriefed, and the two others flew back to Bangkok.

There were some nagging concerns. There were inconsistencies in the stories about how the money ended up in Abidjan and what amounts the controllers had access to. Originally, we were told the money came south from Libya in tanker trucks, and along the way there were variations of that story. Plus the amount of money the asset controllers had access to was growing. Possibly, they were attempting to appeal to the greed factor. Then there were the serial number inconsistencies. Through our research we learned from the currency serial numbers that the boxes of money we were shown had only left the Federal Reserve in New York a few months earlier, well after the coup in Libya.

The presence of the uniformed guards raised more serious questions. The hotel that Majcher was staying at in central Abidjan was located near the Ivory Coast Central Bank, and he observed guards who were wearing the same uniforms as the ones who were present at the box viewings. The provenance of the money seemed even more murky.

When Majcher met with the two asset controllers to discuss details about the handover of the funds, they did not ask questions about what we would do with the money, how it would be laundered, and most importantly, when and where would they be able to draw on the funds.

The asset controllers did say they wanted one of their people on the plane transporting the money, and they did comment on the possibility that he could be thrown out the door at twenty thousand feet. That we understood as a legitimate concern on their part. They were also asking us to pay some of their expenses up front, which was rebuked. Why would we pay for their expenses when they had boxes of $100 bills?

There was now considerable pressure being put on me by the Canadian-Australian duo to execute the pickup. They wanted their payday, which was understandable, but we needed to be methodical and cautious with every detail.

Upon broader inquiry, the team learned of a "bait and switch" scenario being played out in several French West African countries. Military officers were allowed to borrow boxes of money for a short period of time to flash as part of an advanced fee scam. Trusted sources in French West Africa revealed the ruse had started after Gaddafi's removal. The IPSA team also learned they had been the second of two groups who had been shown the assets on the same Monday afternoon. Our team had arrived on a Friday, and the viewing had to be delayed until the Monday when the central bank would reopen.

The presence of uniformed guards in the room where the Libyan money was inspected raised a serious red flag. One would expect less official-looking guardianship from a group of money launderers. The provenance of the money seemed very murky.

It was not clear how the ruse would have played out, but it would not have been pretty. The scenario started out as an opportunity to transport boxes of money out of the area and realize a finder's fee from the Libyan government for our work. When the pickup took place is when things would have gone horribly wrong. The money most certainly would have not been waiting for us at the airport, as we were asked to arrive in the middle of the night when the central bank was closed. The asset controllers had already tried to obtain advanced fee funding from us, which they realized we would not provide. Their next move would be to arrest us upon arrival, and it would then have turned into an extortion scenario where others would be required to pay for our freedom. If we had engaged the ex-British service's mercenaries to do the pickup and, in turn, arranged to have French Foreign Legion personnel on the ground, the whole thing most likely would have resulted in a nasty, violent conclusion.

We later learned that others had been bilked out of considerable amounts of money and criminally charged and jailed. One scenario resulted in a French national, a CEO of an oil company, being defrauded of $48 million on an "advance fee" scam, and then arrested and jailed when attempting to pick up the money. I'm not sure how one could be led that far down the garden path. Most certainly, greed and bad judgment were two key factors that resulted in the Frenchman's demise.

Our street sense, attention to detail, and clear perspective enabled us to deflect the demand for funds storage and fee-customs kickbacks, and to stay out of trouble. The downside was we were out of pocket for close to $100 thousand in operating costs, and there was the distraction from our normal work. The upside was we were involved in a unique experience, no one got hurt, and there was some positive exposure on the lecture circuit.

It was time to get refocused on establishing the London office.

CHAPTER ELEVEN
THE EVOLUTION FROM A PRIVATE TO PUBLIC COMPANY

- Pioneering compliance in a specific industry.
- Developing a niche and being the global leader.
- The highs/lows of business and then exiting.

The Libyan caper sapped considerable energy from me; it actually took a few weeks to get refocused and back on track with the London plan. The travel and juggling communications through the different time zones while handling the cast of characters in Thailand and the Ivory Coast had worn me down. The Libyan caper was an opportunity that had the potential to reward those involved or change lives in a horribly negative way. It was full-on stress over a few months, and a lot of that time I was operating alone, relying on my instincts.

An IPSA office had been established in Marylebone in the West End of London, which has good access to both the City and Canary Wharf. The City is the historical financial center where the Bank of England is located, along with global entities from the financial, insurance, and commodities industries. Canary Wharf is a relatively new financial district located in the East London docklands. It was developed by the Reichmanns through their company Olympia & York, the Toronto family's business. The Reichmanns struck a deal with Prime Minister Thatcher in 1987 to transform the area into a new commercial district that would relieve pressure on the City that is only one square mile in size.

Unfortunately for the Reichmanns, rail and tube access to the docklands was slow in being developed and resulted in the big banks initially not wanting to make the move. This caused Olympia & York significant financial problems. My focus was on developing due diligence clients in both areas, and also in Mayfair, where the hedge fund companies were concentrated. It was a slow, grinding process, but eventually new clients were being brought on board.

In early 2011, around the same time IPSA was launching in London, Eric Major, the HSBC client from Vancouver, took on a new role and moved to Jersey, Channel Islands. Major was now the CEO at Henley & Partners (HP), a significant player in the Immigrant Investor Industry (III). The III involves the issuance of passports by sovereign nations to high-net-worth individuals who are prepared to invest in the economies of the countries offering the opportunity. The offering countries, approximately twelve worldwide, normally have small populations, and this is a way in which they can grow their gross national revenues. HP worked closely with a number of countries in the Caribbean and Europe that had Citizenship by Investment (CBI) programs and, as a former banker, he was keen to develop the compliance side of the industry. Consequently, I would regularly be invited to speak at events in different parts of the world. Plus, I was now making inroads with the government people who were responsible for the management of the programs.

It soon became evident that the due diligence being conducted by the programs was inadequate on many levels. There are specific challenges in every country when conducting due diligence because of cultural, historical, privacy, and access reasons. Conducting due diligence in China can be daunting if you do not understand the process. In China, with a population of 1.5 billion people, there is only a total of approximately one thousand surnames. To know the true identities of individuals, and to keep track of them, the Hukou system was established. This a household registration system that tracks details on the family members. Every Chinese national has an identification number connecting them to their Hukou file. If meaningful due diligence is to be conducted in China, one must first confirm who the individual is through the identification number, and you need to start with the name spelled in Chinese characters. Once completed, the vetting process can commence.

Effective due diligence, for the most part, was not being conducted. Combined with this, the programs were still using a rule-based process rather than a risk-based approach. The outdated, rule-based system was no longer recognized as the best practice. It was based on gathering documents and checking boxes. The risk-based approach analyzes and assesses the risks posed by applicants wanting to obtain a passport. It is a totally different methodology.

ESTABLISHING A GLOBAL BRAND

Having recognized the gaps in the systems, IPSA was positioned to pioneer the compliance component of the Immigrant Investor Industry. Dan Wachtler financed and supported my efforts to further our business in this area, which included providing pro bono training, establishing a professional association, developing a risk matrix to assist with vetting, and generally supporting the countries in their efforts to grow their programs. In a couple of years, IPSA became the primary due diligence service provider for the passport programs in St. Kitts and Nevis (SKN), Dominica, Antigua, St. Lucia, and Malta in Europe. The team in Vancouver had grown from a handful of researchers to twenty-five, speaking twenty-plus different languages. The revenues in Vancouver went from $100 thousand to $1 million per month. It was very heady stuff. IPSA had established a global brand.

Another breakthrough came about after St. Kitts had a couple of negative experiences that tarnished its global image. The perception by the American and Canadian governments was that St. Kitts had historically been issuing passports to undesirables who were using the document for nefarious activities. Consequently, American regulators issued a notice about St. Kitts' passports, and Canada curtailed the country's visa access. SKN established its program in 1983, long before other countries entered into the Citizenship by Investment space and made some mistakes, resulting in a number of matters needing attention. In 2013, I was summoned to a hotel in London where Prime Minister Douglas was staying. Douglas had been leading SKN since 1995; he had been briefed on IPSA and the work we had been doing with the country's Citizenship by Investment vetting team. My advice was to conduct a total review of the program, including historical files, file management systems, personnel, policies, and procedures—virtually a total overhaul of the program. Douglas was acutely aware of a need to revamp the program, and IPSA was engaged.

Over a two-year period that included an election resulting in the first change in government in twenty years, IPSA persevered with a team of people brought in from Vancouver. To conduct the historical file review, some of my former RCMP colleagues were engaged, including Terry Towns, Al Armstrong, and Neil Skippon. It was reassuring to have people of this caliber working on the project. Plus, full-time people from IPSA were tasked with working in St. Kitts, with Karen Kelly shouldering much of the work. An outside consultant, former banker Les Khan, was contracted to manage the project, and eventually he stayed on to run the SKN program.

In the end, twenty-five recommendations were made, and to its credit, the government implemented all of them. The SKN government was able to get the program back on the right track, and its reforms were regarded as an industry success story. Getting the job done for SKN was a long, arduous process, and in the end, we were all pleased with the outcome.

Recently, I was asked by Dr. Kristin Surak, a professor at London School of Economics, to write a chapter on compliance for a Cambridge University Press resource publication named "Rethinking the Boundaries of Belonging." The chapter was coauthored by Mark Corrado, a Vancouver anti-money laundering specialist. Much of the practical input for the chapter came from my Caribbean experiences.

By the end of 2015, IPSA was on a roll. We had gone from being on the brink in 2008 to grossing $30 million in revenues for the third straight year. Vancouver and the international offices were churning out $12 million a year, and the "look-back" work was back up to $20 million per year. One big advantage we had in Vancouver was that our overhead was paid in Canadian dollars, and most of our invoicing was in American dollars. We were making 25-percent-plus on the exchange, giving us a competitive advantage while increasing our net revenues. We managed this with only fifty full-time employees, and with many others doing project work. We had developed a niche in the Immigrant Investor Industry, and the business model was working well.

A DEAL IS HATCHED

IPSA had an advisory board made up of an eclectic group of businesspeople, most of whom were well-known to Wachtler. Joe Grano was one of the stronger personalities on the board. Grano was the former Chairman of UBS Financial Services, and at the time was the CEO of Centurion Holdings. Centurion Holdings provided advisory services to private and public companies. His company leased office space in midtown New York, and IPSA sublet part of the floor. It was a typical high-rise, high-cost, midtown office space. Wachtler split his time between Phoenix where his family lived and New York where IPSA leased an apartment.

Grano was well aware of the revenues being generated by IPSA and approached Wachtler with a proposal. Grano's proposal involved a public company acquiring IPSA by way of offering shares with little cash being exchanged as the public company had minimal revenues or cash for an outright purchase. The carrot was that the public company would be morphed into a cybersecurity service provider and the firm would evolve into a blue-chip company hiring elite people leaving the American military services. The ex-service personnel had unique skill sets and legitimate access to technology that would be in demand by corporations experiencing cyberattacks. Wachtler was the majority IPSA shareholder, with the Keating family holding a minority position, and I was a distant third owner. The deal was consummated. As IPSA had strong brand recognition, the company name was maintained.

The plan worked on some levels. Subject matter experts were hired, and in turn others followed the path to Root 9B, the new entity, eventually being named the top cybersecurity service provider in America. This was an industry position dominated by Firefox perennially until Root 9B came along. As with many American enterprises, Root 9B traded on the OTC board originally but eventually graduated to a NASDAQ listing.

Root 9B went on a hiring spree, and predictably this resulted in a cash bleed. This is where IPSA became instrumental. The revenues being generated by IPSA were required to feed the bigger machine, resulting in IPSA's accounts payable going into serious arrears. This was particularly troublesome for the immigrant investor due diligence work. Most of the work coming in through the passport programs required due diligence to be completed through a network of subcontractors.

Through the years, I was able to establish a global set of reliable, trustworthy people who were critical to the process of providing meaningful reports for clients. Most of the passport work involved vetting applicants from China, the FSU, and the Middle East. IPSA relied on strong subcontractors in the three regions, and everything had been rolling along nicely until the change in ownership. The subcontractors were not being paid on a timely basis, and the amount owed grew consistently every month. This resulted into huge consternation for IPSA as well as the subcontractors who were now, because of the good will established, carrying the load. The business model developed by IPSA in the passport business was now precariously close to being squandered. Root 9B was not curbing its spending and, in some ways, money was being spent foolishly. When the company was eventually listed on NASDAQ, forty Root 9B employees and their significant others were flown to New York for a one-night dinner extravaganza to celebrate. Most flew in from Colorado Springs, where Root 9B was based. IPSA's cash-generating ability was the sole reason Root 9B could continue existing, and such spendthrift behavior was really off base.

I returned to Vancouver in 2014, and after Wachtler moved on to become the COO of Root 9B, I was made President of IPSA International. We had hired Ricardo Gomez, a former IPSA employee, to head up the newly established Miami office, which gave us reach into Latin America. The long-term plan was to grow this office and have it eventually take control of managing the Caribbean work. With the opening of the Miami office, Wachtler and I had accomplished our plan of making IPSA a global firm. We had European coverage (London), Middle Eastern/African coverage (Dubai), Asian coverage (Hong Kong), and now both North and South American coverage was established. My days were long because all the offices, including New York, were direct reports. There were also three direct reports in Vancouver. Most days would start early with phone calls and email communication continuing well into the evenings.

Traveling from Vancouver to the eastern Caribbean is a long slog, twenty hours door-to-door. My normal trip would be to take the "red eye" from Vancouver, arriving in Toronto around six o'clock in the morning, and then getting on a flight to Antigua. From there, I would fly around to the island countries on the regional carrier, Liat. It made much more sense to service the Caribbean from Miami.

CARVING OFF IPSA

The non-payment for the services provided by the subcontractors was exasperating and close to the breaking point. Something needed to change, or there was going to be an implosion. A decision was made to carve out IPSA and put it on the selling block. The sale of IPSA would be handled by Wachtler, but I was also talking to people in the industry. Two firms I had a history with, one from central Canada and one from New York, became suitors, along with Exiger, an up-and-coming New York risk management company.

Exiger was being spearheaded by Michael Beber and Michael Cherkasky, both of whom had worked for the firm Kroll and who were leaders in the industry. Kroll is recognized as one of the top global brands in the risk management industry. The company was started by former Manhattan prosecutor Jules Kroll in the early 1970s. He had the vision and capacity to launch a company that set the standard for the industry. Exiger had been awarded the monitorship of HSBC by the U.S. Department of Justice, to clean up the money laundering problem that the bank had. This was a five-year deal and a big money-maker. Exiger was on an acquisition spree and recognized the value in IPSA's immigrant investor due diligence business model. However, they were not interested in the "look-back" work in the US.

Eventually, Exiger was the only firm that presented an offer that was negotiated. Beber and Cherkasky recognized they could obtain IPSA at a serious discount and carve out the non-American entities they did not want. Wachtler was the primary on the IPSA side and Beber was the primary on the Exiger side. A sales contract included money going to me, some up front, and the remainder on an earn-out basis. I was taking a haircut, as was Wachtler and Root 9B, but I realized it was close to the best deal I was going to get. Wachtler had done his best to look after me as much as possible. The hang-up for me was the employment agreement being offered by Exiger.

In most acquisitions, the major risk for the company doing the acquisition is losing existing revenues. I had developed the majority of the due diligence revenues and had nurtured the client relationships. Exiger wanted me to stay on in Vancouver for two years after the acquisition to help ensure revenue continuity. It had been a fifteen-year roller-coaster ride with IPSA, and the last few years had been especially exhausting. Plus, it quickly became evident to me that I was not a good fit with Exiger. The company had a much different corporate culture than IPSA. Hubris was clearly present, and other than Beber and Cherkasky, most of the other employees were twenty or more years younger than me. Juxtaposed with this fact was that the company was driven mostly by technology, with little interest in where I came from—law enforcement.

THE DEAL CLOSES

In April 2017, we were nearing the eleventh hour. I had engaged my own legal counsel in Vancouver and spent many hours with them over the weekend trying to close out the deal before the deadline, which was twelve o'clock, Sunday night. The last sticking point was how long I was prepared to stay on as an employee. I wanted out after twelve months, and Exiger was asking for twenty-four months. The last two calls with Wachtler, the seller, and Beber, the buyer, were poignant. Wachtler was saying that if the deal did not close, it was unlikely the subcontractors could be paid out, and IPSA would perish. Beber was saying that if I did not accept the terms of the employment contract, the sales agreement would be pulled off the table. In the end, a compromise was negotiated. I would stay on for twelve months as an employee and an additional twelve months as a consultant. The deal was signed off at seven o'clock Sunday night.

I went home to share the news with my wife, and we cracked a bottle of champagne. It was not really a celebration, but rather a feeling of relief that it was all over, and we could turn the page.

My time with Exiger went quickly and for the most part painlessly. The company was interested in maintaining the existing business, which it did; introductions were made to the decision-makers in the different countries.

The business continues to thrive, which pleases me, as there were many good people recruited by IPSA and who were looked after, finding a home with Exiger. As with any acquisition, some moved on.

Not being considered an insider, I was able to sell my NASDAQ shares at around seven dollars each. Root 9B lasted another six months and was acquired by a private equity fund at a huge discount. The last time I checked, the shares were trading at seven cents.

****

Since the sale of IPSA International, and the one year with Exiger, I have been on my own with Marsh Advisory. The pace has been much slower the last couple of years, but there have been a couple of intriguing corruption-and-bribery investigations. The investigations have been focused on municipal government personnel who have been compromised. In the Greater Vancouver area, the property market has been red hot, creating opportunities for many people to make serious money. The amount of money sloshing around has also negatively affected the judgment of some who, for a price, will cross the line that separates legitimate business dealings from those arising out of corruption. The fact that people will allow themselves to be compromised is nothing new; what is different is the apathy of Canadians I come in contact with who seem unconcerned with how some people make their money by gaming the system.

A federal government corruption scandal in 2020 involving the WE Charity that arose during the course of writing this book during the COVID-19 epidemic is a case in point. The brazenness of corruption underlying the charity set a new low for federal politicians and was an eye-opener for me. Equally disturbing is how the scandal was executed with impunity and seen as inconsequential by many Canadians.

A lot has changed since my journey began in 1971, including the denigration of ethics and values in our society.

****

I have some parting words: investigating in an undercover capacity deeply affected my life in many ways. It has been a forty-five-year journey from being trained, doing the jobs, being the trainer, and effectively using the undercover technique I learned along the way in the private sector. The courts in Canada and elsewhere have ruled on many disputed cases; the undercover technique remains one of the most effective methods for gathering evidence on people who behave recklessly with a lack of regard for laws and society. I continue to use the technique selectively. If you are one of those people who choose a roguish path in life to prey on the innocent and bilk the system, my advice to you is: keep your eye on the rearview mirror.

EPILOGUE

I continue to use the undercover technique, and perhaps one day I will be able to tell the story about an international case currently under review. This case has the potential to result in a book on its own merit. It involves money laundering and corruption being perpetrated by people with professional credentials who have developed elaborate schemes to circumvent the system. It has been fascinating to experience the dealings from the inside and view the incredible darkness of people and firms who portray the facade of being legitimate. Again, the driving factor to the greed is to make more money, and it begs the question: How much money does a person need?

The RCMP Undercover Program is still viable, and people continue to be trained. Sadly, fewer people want to make the commitment to this type of work, and thus it is becoming difficult to fill the courses with undercover trainees. I believe this is a reflection on the type of people joining the RCMP. It has never been a path for the timid, and often it is not seen as a career-enhancing move.

The techniques learned and honed have been instrumental in contributing to my successes while I pursued my goals. I would not change any of it and recommend it to others, if you fit the mold.

FURTHER READING

Burgis, Tom. *KLEPTOPIA: How Dirty Money is Conquering the World.* HarperCollins Publishers, 2020.

Burgis, Tom. "Tower of Secrets: the Russian Money Behind a Donald Trump Skyscraper." *Financial Times*, 11 Jul. 2018.

CBC News. *Tobacco firms to pay $550M over smuggling.* 13 Apr. 2010. https://www.cbc.ca/news/canada/tobacco-firms-to-pay-550m-over-smuggling-1.902510.

Edwards, Peter, and Michel Auger. *The Encyclopedia of Canadian Organized Crime: from Captain Kidd to Mom Boucher.* McClelland & Stewart, 2012.

Farnsworth, Clyde H. "Russians Are Coming, but for Money." *New York Times*, 3 Oct. 1993.

Harris, Michael. *The Judas Kiss: The Undercover Life of Patrick Kelly.* McClelland & Stewart, 1995.

Hollingsworth, Mark, and Stewart Lansley. *Londongrad: From Russia with Cash: The Inside Story of the Oligarchs.* Fourth Estate, 2010.

Keenan, Kouri, and Joan Brockman LL. *Mr. Big: Exposing Undercover Investigations in Canada.* Fernwood Pub. Co. Ltd., 2010.

Lamothe, Lee, and Adrian Humphreys. *The Sixth Family: The Collapse of the New York Mafia and the Rise of Vito Rizzuto*. HarperCollins Publishers, 2014.

Macklem, Katherine. "WestJet, Air Canada Spy on Each Other." *The Canadian Encyclopedia*, 14 Oct. 2004, www.thecanadianencyclopedia.ca/en/article/westjet-air-canada-spy-on-each-other.

Manthrope, Jonathan. *Restoring Democracy in an Age of Populists & Pestilence*. Cormorant Books, 2020.

"Mafia lawyer remembered on 25th anniversary of his murder." *Montreal Gazette*, 13 May 2016. https://montrealgazette.com/news/local-news/mafia-lawyer-remembered-on-25th-anniversary-of-his-murder.

"Recovering stolen assets: Making a hash of finding the cash." *The Economist*, 11 May 2013, www.economist.com/international/2013/05/11/ making-a-hash-of-finding-the-cash.

Ward, Andrew. "Antonov rails at 'prejudices.'" *Financial Times*, 25 Feb. 2010, behind a paywall at https://www.ft.com/content/837265ee-2244-11df-9a72-00144feab49a.

Watts, Richard. "FISHBOAT DRUG BUSTS: Court upholds prison sentences in global smuggling scheme." *Times Colonist*, Victoria, British Columbia, 12 Sept. 2006.